Polish Architecture in Contemporary Innovation
Thoughts, Dreams and Places

Nina Juzwa and Jakub Świerzawski

Edited by Nina Juzwa

LONDON AND NEW YORK

First published in English 2024
by Routledge
4 Park Square, Milton Park, Abingdon, Oxon OX14 4RN

and by Routledge
605 Third Avenue, New York, NY 10158

Routledge is an imprint of the Taylor & Francis Group, an informa business

Published in Polish as Myśli, Marzenia, Miejsca. Architektura polska we współczesnej innowacyjności

© Nina Juzwa, Jakub Świerzawski, 2021

© Narodowy Instytut Architektury i Urbanistyki, 2021

Copyright for the English translation © Szczepan Witaszek

The right of Nina Juzwa and Jakub Świerzawski to be identified as authors of this work has been asserted in accordance with sections 77 and 78 of the Copyright, Designs and Patents Act 1988.

All rights reserved. No part of this book may be reprinted or reproduced or utilised in any form or by any electronic, mechanical, or other means, now known or hereafter invented, including photocopying and recording, or in any information storage or retrieval system, without permission in writing from the publishers.

Trademark notice: Product or corporate names may be trademarks or registered trademarks, and are used only for identification and explanation without intent to infringe.

British Library Cataloguing-in-Publication Data
A catalogue record for this book is available from the British Library

ISBN: 978-1-032-51772-8 (hbk)
ISBN: 978-1-032-53784-9 (pbk)
ISBN: 978-1-003-41356-1 (ebk)

DOI: 10.4324/9781003413561

Typeset in Times New Roman
by Apex CoVantage, LLC

Contents

Instead of an Introduction   vii

Introduction   1

Part I The Continuity of Thought in Architecture   6
   Kept in Memory   6
      The Masters   7
      Diversity of Creative Attitudes   8
      The Time of Computers   10
   The Search for Contemporaneity   14
      Geometrical Haughtiness and New Materiality   15
   Idea, Design, Architect   18
      The Design Process   18
      Architects – The Creators Speak with Their Own Words   21
   Discourse on Architectural Space   26
      The Creation of Architectural Form   26
      Ecstatic Architecture   27
      "Wowhouse"   29
      Rationalism or Emotions   36
   Diversity and Surprise   38
      On Creativity   38
      Concept, Context, Content   41

Part II Value, Beauty, and Place   48
   On User-Friendly Architecture: Three Examples   48
   On Value and Beauty in Architecture   52

Value 52
Beauty 56
Understanding Beauty 56
Searching for Beauty in Architecture 59
Place 62
Space and Place 62

Part III Presentation of Polish Examples 88
Introduction 88
Office Buildings 91
Courthouses 111
Museums 117
Cultural Facilities 125
Houses of Music 133
Sports Facilities 145
Educational Facilities 149
Libraries 161
Churches 167

Conclusion 175
Architecture and Art 175

Bibliography *181*
Index *191*

Instead of an Introduction

The outstanding book by Nina Juzwa and Jakub Świerzawski, which you, the reader, are currently holding in your hands, does not need an introduction. It speaks for itself. It is only because of the responsibility of the publisher and the gratitude of the reader that I will allow myself just a few remarks.

Architecture is the art of transforming space. It is also an art of writing about architecture. A difficult art, since it is a field that combines beauty and science. On one hand, it is shaped by existential humanist thought; on the other, it must be built in such a way as to be experienced (Steen Eiler Rasmussen). These aspects are connected and mutually condition each other. This is how this book was written. On one hand, it contains musings on the continuity of thought in architecture, ideas, public space, geometry, rationalism, and emotions; on the other, examples of completed structures, which are an example of the established theoretical assumptions. Architecture is, above all, the art of building.

Writing about architecture is difficult. Most of the publications are either the fragmentary musings of columnists or the incomprehensible hermetic scientific reflections on such an abstract level that they no longer have anything to do with humanities. Yet the authors of this book, without abandoning scientific ambitions, speak of architecture in an easy-to-understand way and, at the same time, avoid lapsing into journalism. However, this does not mean that the book is an easy read, because the thoughts on beauty and wisdom of space are a domain of the theory and critique of architecture and not journalism.

The authors quote a classic of hermeneutics: "beautiful things are those whose value is of itself evident" (Hans-Georg Gadamer). This is a definition of the phenomenological reception of space – after all, Gadamer was a student of Martin Heidegger. As we have said, architecture is experienced. The multitude of dimensions of its impact makes it difficult to conduct multilayered scientific, humanist reflections (Juhani Pallasmaa). On the other hand, in a direct experience of space, its holistic reception is obvious, despite the fact that it is a unique experience. Tadao Andō – one of the most outstanding architects of the twentieth century – used to say that very seldom, when he was faced with an architectural structure, was he convinced that he was dealing with a work of art.

Nina Juzwa and Jakub Świerzawski, in presenting carefully selected examples, show how the "defined by them" values of ideation of space are implemented. This internally diverse constellation is at the same time extremely cohesive. It shows how many different values are part of urban planning and architecture, to ultimately provide a beautiful and wise space, which "is not part of the necessities of life but is concerned with the 'how' of life" (Hans-Georg Gadamer).

Among the categories that are found in the book of particular significance seem to be "people-friendly places" (value, beauty, and place). This is a new perception of space in accordance with the Baukultur–Davos Declaration, signed by the Ministers of Culture of EU states in 2018. "Starchitecture," which is created based on the principle of "fuck the context" (Rem Koolhass), has more and more opponents among architects. Respect for place and local community has acquired primary significance a decade after the publication of *The Architectural Review* with the essays of Peter Buchanan ("The Big Rethink," 2011–2012) as well as his "Empty Gestures: Starchitecture's Swan Song" (2015). In it, he wrote: "Architecture, once the encompassing mother of the arts, completed by painting and sculpture and carrier of cultural significance and meaning, has become reduced to superfluous spectacle." We can also see this in Poland, at every step finding our own "icons of Starchitecture," promoted by the commercial media. The "swan song" as the last stage of postmodernism (the baroque of modernism) is to be the harbinger of wise architecture, thanks to which it is also to be beautiful. Its wisdom will be counted in "carbon footprints" and a positive influence on the life of the local community, which is part of the postulates of the aforementioned Baukultur. It is also a confirmation of the thesis – a postulate of Romano Guardini – that every age should find its synthesis of nature and culture, whereby Guardini sees that from the moment of the appearance of man, nature has changed, and both its definition as well as its relations with culture are constantly evolving.

Will academic theoreticians and architecture critics, and along with them creators, change their approach to transforming space, as Buchanan expects?

Certainly, we will be convinced by the enthusiasts of subsequently appearing trends that after the salvific deconstructivism comes an even more necessary parametric design, or parametricism.[1] And then another . . . *ism*. Just as is the case with fashion. I am a pessimist when it comes to overcoming these weaknesses of architecture, despite the fact that the last Pritzker Award (Anne Lacaton, Jean-Philippe Vassal, 2021) clearly points towards the desired trend of changes. More and more often we can hear of a "new paradigm of building," although it is quite seldom that understandable theses appear.[2]

It can also be noted that the book by Nina Juzwa and Jakub Świerzawski is perhaps the first academic/critical publication showing such a wide spectrum of Polish architecture of the last 30 years, thanks to which it may serve as a

Instead of an Introduction ix

sort of a guide. This is an extremely important aspect – especially at a time of migratory education and "architectural tourism."

It is also worth appreciating the mastery of writing about such a difficult topic. Here nothing is left up to chance – the book is well-thought-out and appealing in every detail. The drawings of the plans and cross sections of the presented structures are also very important. Private conceptual sketches or design drawings show the specificity of the world of architecture. They also provide an insight into the true workshop of "architectural matter" (Dariusz Kozłowski).

This is a concept and implementation fit for outstanding architects.

Bolesław Stelmach
Head of the National Institute
for Architecture and Urban Planning

Notes

1 See, for example, P. Schumacher, *The Autopoiesis of Architecture*, New York 2011.
2 See, for example, C. Bielecki, *Sztuka budowania. Nowy paradygmat*, Warszawa 2013.

Introduction

The book is a story about buildings that were created in Poland between 1980 and 2019. These architectural events are shown with world trends as a backdrop. While writing the book, we kept in mind the words of Georg Gadamer: "Everything that is not part of the necessities of life but is concerned with the 'how.' . . . Beautiful things are those whose value is of itself evident."[1] Admiring the iconic events of contemporary architecture, we mainly refer to structures which are harmoniously incorporated into their surroundings, thus creating user-friendly architecture.

The three parts of the book are based on a simple pattern:

- Part I, titled "Continuity of Thought in Architecture," focuses on the problem of creating and shaping architectural form. In it, we also undertake the dialogue on the subject of the creation of form, while posing the question of why the *Pritzker Prize* is important.
- Part II, titled "Value, Beauty, and Place in Architecture," is an attempt to respond to *the* question of how architecture can change the image of a place. The answer consists of examples of user-friendly architecture, value, and beauty in architecture, place.
- Part III, "Example Presentation," shows buildings that were created in contemporary Poland. We list them in groups according to their function, pointing out forms that were inspired by the culture of the region, the historical culture of the place, or those which are a new quality and are the foundation of the creation of a place.
- The *Conclusion* stops at the attempt to show the relations between architecture and art which exist in the area of the feelings and actions of the designer.

Innovativeness in architecture can take on many forms. Most frequently, these are buildings that are far removed from the principles of right-angle geometry, whose formal solutions take advantage of new possibilities of construction

DOI: 10.4324/9781003413561-1

and new materiality of the construction materials. The goal here is to take advantage of the effect of surprise or to achieve the impression of weightlessness of matter. It is meant to cause an effect of lightness for the normally enormous building. Attempting to better define the phenomena of innovativeness in contemporary architecture, we could speak of a concentration of expressionist tendencies, as well as of a wider use of the contemporary possibilities of technology in shaping architectural form.[2] The *innovativeness*, which is part of the title, is a fashionable word, which is also associated with architecture. In technology, it is most often understood as the principles of interpretation of a new improved product or service. It can also concern a new organizational method in economy, organization of the place of work, or in relations with surroundings. Innovativeness, therefore, can pertain to a product but may also pertain to a process or the technology of product manufacturing. In the case of architecture, innovativeness is best visible in the shaping of form, in architectural geometry, or new materiality.

Speaking of innovativeness in architecture is connected with the wider application, in civil engineering, and also in shaping the architecture, of methods derived from sciences, to which the knowledge and talent of the architect-designer are added. These are also used in making calculations, in drawings, in carrying out experiments, in accelerating the development of technical solutions, and in the creation of systemic solutions. The development of urban communities that accompanies this phenomenon means the creation of new needs, and thus the construction of new buildings, often with a complicated structure, which introduce new functionality into building design.

Considering the problem of *modernity and novelty* in art, Karolina Tulkowska-Słyk[3] supports herself on a text regarding innovation in business by Everett M. Rogers.[4] He notes that at every step of the decision-making process, there is a search for innovation, and either a new solution is accepted as the best possible one or those that do not fulfill this criterion are discarded.

A truly new idea is short-lasting and generally is subjective. Its duration depends on its "freshness" in the eyes of recipients. Thus, innovation "contains within the opposite of progress, in which the new is at the same time necessary and impossible."[5] The author defines *innovation* as an "idea, practice, or object that is perceived as new by an individual or group."[6]

In the context of considering general civilizational changes, Karolina Tulkowska-Słyk considers the pattern of the development of innovative concepts that is similar to the needs of designing in architecture and urban design, pointing out subsequent steps:

- The *intellectual stage* – meaning, the creation of a new idea.
- The *technical stage* – during which the possibility of applying a new idea and persuasion occurs at the crossways of thought and the area of the application of the idea.

- The *social stage* – during which a collaboration develops between the initiators, implementers, and recipients.
- The *final stage* – *confirmation*, when the concept is verified over time.

She also points out the criteria that must be fulfilled to approve a novel solution. These are:

- Superiority over an existing solution, which points to the relative advantage as far as function, construction, material, esthetics, solutions.
- Matching existing norms as far as usage and competencies of the executive apparatus.
- Complexity, meaning, showing the possibility of implementation, without worsening or with improvement to the designing conditions, implementation, and utilization of the building.
- Accessibility, expressed in characteristics understandable to the recipient, leading to intuitive usage.[7]

Of equal importance for the topic in question is a book titled *The Art Instinct: Beauty, Pleasure, and Human Evolution*.[8] The author, Denis Dutton, suggests creating a theoretical apparatus useful for the needs of the multi-thematic, intercultural world of art. He proposes a universal interpretation based on distinguishable "specific traits," which he calls "recognizable criteria," underlining the interdisciplinary and multi-thematic character of works of art. He writes that the specificity of this field allows for the connection in art, various traditions, and genres, but also the inclusion of personal experiences of the artist. "The art combining fantasy and emotions, fuses these factors together, then transform them in the esthetic imagination of the creator."[9] Similar features characterize the work of the architect-designer. The terms "new," "novel," and "innovative," in the musings of architecture theoreticians, usually appear in the description in situations of controversy in face of the universally approved intellectual concepts.

The usage of the name "contemporary innovativeness" is a result of thoughts and discussions on the subject, where we wanted to emphasize the time and place in which our thoughts find themselves, but also "beautiful art of architecture," considered in the general civilizational development.

Part I discusses design thoughts and ideas in contemporary architecture. Examples of world and Polish architecture are an illustration that shows subsequent conceptual assumptions in the architecture of recent years. **Part II** discusses Polish examples that changed the character of a place. The examples of the Oslo Opera and the Museum of Contemporary Art in New York depict how architecture can "tame" the urban space. The third example, concerning the transformation of a post-industrial area in Lower Lusatia,[10] shows how, in taking advantage of the exceptional beauty of non-functioning mining devices, they can be converted into art. In **Part III**, we present examples of

Polish architecture, which started our discussions, becoming their principal element.

The main reason for our reflections on the topic of architecture is public utility buildings, yet there are also facilities with a different function. We created this story thanks to coming face-to-face with architecture, which astounds us, which makes us anxious, and which moves us.

In part, the subjective character of the selection of the examples provided is obvious. It is an expression of trust in our views and is not connected with the want to classify or compare. It is important that we establish a general principle to describe the examples that we "have touched," seen *in situ*. Although we were not able to fully implement this principle, it worked for the greater part of the facilities.

Here it is necessary to thank the creators of the described buildings for a rapid response to our request to supply drawings and photographs for the book. We would also like to thank the whole NIAiU team for their collaboration in creating this book.

> Personally, I would like to thank Kuba Świerzawski, my partner in creating the book, for his cooperation in the constant discussions and actions connected with writing the text and searching for materials. It seems that these last two years concluded in friendship and the feeling of fulfillment. I would also like to thank my family, Maja and Andrzej, for their understanding; my granddaughter Dominika for her help and involvement in creating and supplementing the photographic documentation. Thanks are also in order for the "architectural kids," Filip, Marta, and Paulina, for their drawings of the presented structures, and Martyna, whose love for books has led us to discover amazing texts about art.
>
> Finally . . . *last but not the least*, I am grateful to all my friends who believed in me and supported me. I would like to thank all the professors – my beloved Halusia Dunin-Woyseth, who was in constant contact with me, despite living in distant Norway; Bolek Stelmach, Wojtek Bonenberg, and Janek Słyk; as well as Tomasz Konior. Friendly discussions allowed me to put in order the world of my thoughts. Thank you!
>
> Nina Juzwa

> I would like to thank Nina Juzwa for the opportunity to work together, the constant help, and the friendship. I am grateful that for so many years she has been willing to share her knowledge, experience, and the joy of creating. I would also like to thank Martyna for her support, understanding, and sense. . . . The kindness, sympathy, and support of many people give me strength and the drive to work. I thank my mom, my brother Jan, family, and friends.
>
> Jakub Świerzawski

Notes

1 H. G. Gadamer, *Truth and Method*, Warsaw 2013, translated by B. Baran, p. 472.
2 This assumption also references the Davos Conference, during which in January 2018, European countries signed a declaration to promote high-quality civil engineering culture based on recognizing the importance of cultural factors. The concept of European culture requires the integration of the resources of knowledge and ability with innovative technique.
3 Karolina Tulkowska-Słyk, *Nowoczesne mieszkanie*, Warsaw 2019.
4 E. M. Rogers, *Diffusion of Innovation*, New York 2010, p. 202.
5 Ibid.
6 Ibid.
7 Ibid., p. 36.
8 Denis Dutton, *The Art. Instinct. Beauty, Pleasure and Human Evolution*, transl. by J. Luty, Cracow 2019.
9 Ibid., pp. 10–26.
10 The area situated between Berlin and Dresden, not far from Cottbus, near the city of Grossraeschen. The mining industry located here supplied coal to industries as well as the urbanized areas of Berlin.

Part I The Continuity of Thought in Architecture

Looking at an empty piece of paper, on which the first words about architectural contemporaneity are to be written, we are filled with thoughts of the shaping of form in architecture. When they are put in order, they create a series of titles: "Kept in Memory," "The Search for Contemporaneity," "Idea, Design, Architect," "Discourse on Architectural Space."

Kept in Memory

Thought, matter, and place are three basic elements of architecture that tell the story of life, human needs, and dreams – three elements that are a transmitter of communications between generations and also between societies.

Ancient buildings were always situated in a spot that was beautiful, important, often not easily accessible – magnificent Gothic cathedrals, excellent in their proportions; city squares of the Middle Ages and Renaissance; illusionary palaces and gardens of the Baroque. Places thanks to which architecture allows us to better experience our history. Their meaning in the development of culture signifies more than an ever-growing excellence of technical solutions and an evolution of architectural thought. It means that the changing forms of human existence influence not only the change in human needs but also the way the architectural beauty of buildings is perceived.

In architecture, similarly to culture, the present means that in our memory we also have a recollection of buildings that were built in the past. However, when we create a projection of the image of the future, we see both the present world, which exists around us, as well as the previous, historical one. This all-encompassing memory allows us to create new places and forms in an architectural image.

Likewise, when we want to speak of the innovativeness of contemporary architecture, we must go back in time to recall buildings that were the harbinger of this contemporaneity. Today's innovativeness would not have been possible if not for architects, for whom the driving force behind their creation was the want to break the stereotype about that which is already in existence, which is traditional, and that which is new and different.

DOI: 10.4324/9781003413561-2

The Masters

Here we must speak about the works of two great masters of recent years: the Fallingwater in Pennsylvania and the Guggenheim Museum in New York, by F. L. Wright, and the Notre Dame du Haut pilgrim chapel in Rochamp or the La Tourette Priory on the slopes of the Massif Centrale, by Le Corbusier.

Saint-Marie-de-la-Tourette Priory Eveux-Sur-Abresle, 1956–1960, by Le Corbusier, with the aid of the musician Iannis Xenakis, stands on the slopes of the Massif Centrale. It is the last of the grand structures built by the great Corbu, and one of 17 of his works which are on the UNESCO Cultural and Natural Heritage list.

In designing the priory, Corbusier possessed complete freedom in selecting the location and the form of the structure. The only hint given to him by the prior of the Dominican Fathers was: "create a silent, voiceless place, which can accommodate one hundred bodies and one hundred souls."[1] And thus a square building was created with an internal atrium and an enormous grass roof. The mighty, reinforced concrete walls with a row of windows finished off with sculptures soar high above the idyllic, mountainous landscape of the Massif Centrale. Only the simple body of the church has an entrance, directly from the ground. The priory itself, the refectory, the library, the dining room, and the monks' living quarters are all above ground level. The interior is simple and filled with coldness, which is slightly lessened by the light that enters the building. Inside, many details point to the ingeniousness of the author. The Fathers' cells are situated on the last story, with a distinct, elongated shape, and fulfill all the guidelines of *The Modulor*. The decreasing number of monks has provided the opportunity to accommodate secular seekers of silence, pilgrimages of architecture students, and enthusiasts of the master.

The pilgrimage chapel Notre Dame du Haut in Rochamp and the La Tourette Priory are an expression of architectural thought of the middle twentieth century. The structures are deeply rooted in the culture of their time period, present formal perfection, and are an expression of what we can call architectural beauty. Corbu himself spoke thus of the La Tourette: "I attempted to create a place for meditation, study, and prayer for the brothers. The commission was to design living quarters for monks, at the same time ensuring them with that which contemporary people need the most – peace and quiet."[2] The lonely, enormous structure built out of concrete and glass is a place. A place full of peace, thoughtfulness, but also the joy of existence. When during the quiet hours of the early evening we look upon the hilly landscape surrounding the convent, perhaps we will be able to see scenes similar to those that appear on the landscapes of Bruegel the Elder.

Guggenheim Museum in New York, 1956–1959, by Frank Lloyd Wright. When writing about contemporary architectural innovativeness, the building of the Guggenheim Museum is worth mentioning. Wright "an arrogant celebrity" and a charismatic genius of modernism, discards the ideas of Le Corbusier, the cold functionalism of modernist architecture. Instead of machine buildings, he suggests "organic architecture combined with nature."[3] The foundation for the construction of the Guggenheim Museum in New York, which would house *non-objective painting* and was to bring to light the ideas of paintings by Kandinsky, Mondrian, and other defiant artists, was established in 1937. The building itself was completed after the war and was opened six months after the death of its creator. Its founders wanted it to show the world the thoughts and dreams of artists, who must often break through the standard image of art.

The idea accompanying the creation of the foundation can be seen in the formal concept of the building. In form, the Guggenheim is reminiscent of a rolled-up white ribbon, widening towards the top. The spiral interior, shaped thus, is covered with a glass dome. A relatively high (70 meters) building stands near the green areas of Central Park. It is situated in distinct opposition to the nineteenth-century standard beauty of the building of the Metropolitan Museum of Art.

The architectural geometry of Guggenheim does not honor the traditional, established forms of the prestigious structure. This was done purposefully by F. L. Wright, who wanted the nearby lordly building of the Met to lose its lordliness, to be reminiscent of a "Protestant barn"[4] when compared to the new museum. This concept is also seen in the interior. The dome does not introduce a sufficient amount of light inside, while the roundness of the walls is not the best form of exposing flat paintings. Hung on lines sticking out from the wall, they do not make the exposition any easier. The building was criticized from its very inception. The geometrical but also the functional rebellious nature of the building did not initially meet with general approval. However, the museum became an icon of the city and today is one of the most desirable museum spaces in New York.

In the years 2005–2008, it was renovated. In 1992, a new, higher tower was added to the building, which was heavily criticized. Despite some objections about architectural solution of the function that serves the presentation and storage of paintings, the beauty of the place still seems to be undeniable. The first to appreciate it was the film industry. It has been used in numerous films to underline the dramaturgy of scenes.[5]

The works of masters of modernism which have been recalled here and which are deeply rooted in the culture of their times were an architectural challenge for the future. Both possess an everlasting characteristic of excellence, while their function, situated outside the trend of everyday needs and events, causes them to become art in the discussion on architectural innovativeness, as they radiate with the creativity of their creators.

Diversity of Creative Attitudes

In the period between 1920 and 1970, Charles Jencks distinguished six principal traditions.[6] These, subject to the conditions of the socio-political movement, show the relations between architecture and the possibilities of technique and technology of construction. The author refers to these creative attitudes of architects as movement or tradition. It seems valid to remind ourselves of the more prominent ideas and principles that were the foundation of the architectural present.

As the author of *Modern Movements in Architecture* writes, the tradition of idealism has, since the twenties of the twentieth century until contemporary times, been that, which is universally considered "modern architecture." The ideas and thoughts of this tradition consist of both social ideas, liberal humanism, and rather vaguely defined utopia. The architects gathered around such ideas believed they needed to present a different vision of social order. However, not concentrating on the social premises of changes, they attempted, "in line with Platonic idealists . . . to bring their buildings to such excellence as if they would represent some fundamental cosmic order."[7]

The initial founders of the modern architecture movement included Le Corbusier, Mies van der Rohe, and Walter Gropius, as well as, later, Aldo van Eyck, Louis Kahn, James Stirling, and others. The painter-polemicist and architect Theo van Doesburg, referring to the cult of the machine of the first modernists, explains this striving for social liberation in political categories thusly:

[I]t concerns not only the aspect of the machine as a tool which saves time, but it also encompasses its universal and abstract quality. Since the machine is impersonal it brings certain equality among people and leads the evolution of art in the direction of abstraction and universalism . . . the implementation of a collective style by a joint effort and in accordance with a joint concept.[8]

The social utopia which is present in the works of architects gathered in CIAM broke down in the 1950s when esthetics triumphed under the moniker of international style.

The movement referred to by Jencks as the tradition of self-consciousness developed during the time of the establishment of pro-Fascist movements in Europe. Architecture is dependent on those who manage politics and the economy. This characteristic caused it to play a rather shameful role in history, striving to justify great luminaries of architecture who accepted commissions for buildings that had little to do with humanism or social idealism.

This trend mainly manifested itself in the completion of governmental facilities or buildings for the newly created economic corporations.[9] The attitude of the creators of the early years of modernism was characterized by an obsessive attachment to works of old patterns of architecture. The submissiveness towards the past, as Charles Jencks notes, was to be a measure of earthly immortality. We can find this both in the faith of August Perret in the universal characteristics of classical architecture as well as in the idea of Adolf Hitler, who trusted in the classical tradition of the thousand-year-old Third Reich.[10] Many well-known architects took on commissions from the government. In once again recalling *Modern Movements in Architecture*, we can, not without satisfaction, state that these "buildings which were to ensure the immortality of their creators became so similar to one another, that they were forgotten."[11]

Supersensualists came to be from the connection of elements of intuition and tradition on the level of formalism and fashion. This movement can be compared to Art Nouveau from the turn of the centuries. Moreover, it very clearly referenced the "economic miracle" which occurred in Italy at that time. This is even more visible in art, in the formal features seen in the cult film by Federico Fellini *Dolce Vita*.

The tradition of logic is a trend that developed in Japan. Its leader was Kenzo Tange. As Jencks noted, it was characteristic that Japanese architects, in taking over ideas from numerous sources, systematically improve on them, making them better than the original.[12] A sort of a "trademark" of this tradition was to underline the significance of systematic planning. It was followed by computer techniques,[13] where the next step was the development of a parametric design. Models created at that time were a natural result of team design.

Simultaneously to the development of team design, manifests were created, which were a direct opposition to such attitudes. This was the case with Hundertwasser, who defended the freedom of the individual creator. "Only when the architect, mason, and user are one, meaning one and the same person, can we talk about architecture. Everything else is not architecture but an embodiment of a crime."[14] Charles Jencks compares the creative approaches of an architect of the mid-twentieth century to changes that exist in nature in the process of evolution of species. However, the tradition of thought in architecture does not become completely extinct. There is always a possibility of a rebirth of form or initial idea. In addition, architect-designers have a tendency to jump from one of the aforementioned genres to another, arbitrarily mixing forms and ideas. In this way, new forms and ideas are often created.[15]

The visible diversity of creative approaches causes an obvious difficulty in classifying creators. Such was the foundation for the creation of the diagram of Charles Jencks that expresses the diversity of creative thought in architecture.

The Time of Computers

The following years were for designing in architecture, a time of yet another breakthrough in the development of thoughts. It became a period of the development of digitalization and computer culture. Even if the thought of the designer still remains the principal element of the concept of architecture, new design tools gain importance. On the other hand, the evaluation of the quality of architecture had lost the feature of principles in force in exchange for a more and more common relativism.

At the turn of the twentieth and twenty-first centuries, environment-friendly techniques and technologies became the dominant strategy. Contemporary horizons of the development of technical culture are outlined by a wave of new figures in architectural creation. At the same time, an almost-unimaginable development of technology influences the creation of structures, which take advantage of this development in a more and more creative way.

Richard Buckminster Fuller (1895–1983) searched for energy-saving solutions allowing for the creation of large coverings. He developed the concept of geo-domes. Experiments with artificial materials contributed to the search for residential building solutions in the shape of domes. For example, in 1941, Edwin Wallace Neff (1895–1982) used an inflated balloon as a formwork for the concrete *bubble houses*.[16]

An architect who designed complex geometrical concrete shells was Eero Saarinen (1910–1961). Together with the engineers from Ammann and Whitney, he designed the terminal of the TWA Flight Center in New York. His concept was for architecture to emphasize the emotions of passengers. He wanted to achieve such an effect by using a uniform language of forms in the whole building. In 1959, Saarinen wrote:

> All the roundness, all the rooms and elements of interior decoration, all the way to the shape of the sings, information boards, balustrades, and check-in desks, should exhibit a uniform character. We want the passenger, who is walking down the corridor, to feel as if he would find himself in completely changed surroundings, where one thing is the result of another and belongs to the common world of forms.[17]

The roundness of the New York Terminal is a result of strict cooperation between architects and constructors. The roof consists of four double-curved shells. Their thickness oscillates between 20 cm and 1.1 m.[18] This curved line arrangement gives off an impression of an organic whole. The protrusions and flexures are not only reminiscent of sculpture decorations but also fulfill a civil engineering task – they stiffen the shells of the roof. Their edges create ribs that strengthen the whole construction and transport the loads towards the supports. The shells are separated from each other by a crack that lets light into the building interior and rest on four common supports with a shape reminiscent of the letter *Y*. The whole has an organic and free character.[19] Curt Siegel believed that "this form is completely free of geometrical bonds. We do not notice circular lines, right angles, or parabolas. Here, we have new forms and new proportions."[20]

The structure was criticized for lack of functionality, which lowered its utility comfort and for problems with advanced technologies.[21] To design the shape of the roof, clay and cardboard models were used, both for the exterior and interior of the building. The shapes and sizes of the supports were a result of construction calculations.[22] Saarinen carefully analyzed problems from different fields; often, to then find an exceptional form or construction expressing the architectural concept,[23] he searched for solutions in modern technologies. The terminal building was also closed down in 2021. Currently, the icon of architectural contemporaneity is to function as a hotel in the so-called system of "boutique hotels, combining fashion and design."[24]

Frei Otto (1925–2015) used models to study statics and geometry and to perfect the method of construction calculations. He used models made out of soap bubbles and hanging models to find optimal forms. He developed modern light tent, rope, pneumatic, and hydraulic constructions, as well as mobile roofs – umbrellas. Taking into account the economics and ecology, he attempted to find various ways of their use. Since the 1950s of the twentieth century, he had built complex models, looking for the perfect tension. Models provided him with the basic information about form,[25] and based on this, the engineers in Otto's workshop performed one of the first computer analyses of designs of civil engineering constructions in architecture.[26] In his studies on construction, he collaborated with architects, designers, but also biologists. This interdisciplinary activity allowed for a better understanding of the functioning of forms and biological structures[27] which were used in shaping form in architecture.

It was decided that Frei Otto would design the German pavilion for the World Expo in 1967. He was to show innovativeness in the architecture of post-war Germany. The size of the structure was approximately 8,000 m², and its construction consisted of a steel net hung on eight masts, which were spread out at irregular distances. The masts, connected with anchored cables, were outside the structure. A transparent polyester material was put on a steel net, which created a great tent. The construction of the pavilion took six weeks.[28] In order to complete the design, a complicated hanging model was created.[29]

In 1968, Otto Frei participated in the design of the hanging structures that made up the canopy of the Olympic Stadium in Munich, invented by Günther Behnisch. The roof over the stadium created an "umbrella" also "over the landscape."[30] The architect developed larger and larger design models, and Fritz Leonhardt and Wolfhart Andrä worked on the design using CAD programs.[31] The masts that support the rope net, covered with panels from dimmed acrylic, constitute supports for the covering – a great roof. The roof itself is reminiscent of a cloud, one that floats over the landscape. The great hanging form is also a covering for the stadium stands, a sports hall, as well as the Olympic swimming pool. The curvilinear roof of the covering of the stadium almost symbolically floats over the stands, which are built in a crater left over from the Second World War.[32] The design was extremely novel, both in its esthetic solutions as well as in the concept of the material utilized. The formal solution of the "roof" is still novel and even now is an expression of geometric pride. The curvilinearity of the structure floating over the stadium became an inspiration for the concept of solutions of parametric architecture.[33]

The high-tech architecture in its form emphasized the significance of relations, which are a result of design solutions, and a result of the installation furnishing of the building. This approach is visible in one of the most famous examples from this period, the *Centre National d'Art et de la Culture Georges Pompidou* in Paris by Renzo Piano and Richard Rogers. The frame of the building is visible on the external image and causes the building to be reminiscent of a "living organism without an external covering." It looks as if "the entrails of the building," generally carefully hidden, are ostensibly visible here, creating an architectural beauty. This sensation is heightened by the concept of placing escalators inside glass tubes, which, attached to the elevation, bring to mind associations with the interior of a technical device, or a building-machine.

Fascination with novelty "in itself" is visible in Lloyd's building in London by Richard Rogers or the Bank of Hong Kong building as well as the Bank of Shanghai in Hong Kong, both designed by Norman Foster.

Another approach characterized the Archigram group. Its members published curvilinear designs representing inflated structures, created out of artificial materials. These designs were not completed but had an influence on the then generation of architects.[34]

In subsequent trends of avant-garde architecture, deconstructivism was an influential movement. It included creators such as Daniel Libeskind, Zaha Hadid, or Frank Gehry.[35] For this architecture, non-typical form was of primary importance. The architecture of deconstructivism was a manifestation of novelty and formal diversity. Its important feature was a conscious striving for the breakthrough of habits and emotions connected with the reception of an architectural image.

One of the first architects who used new ideas was Peter Eisenman. He created designs of buildings with straight-line forms in which there are inwardly and outwardly curved surfaces. Oval, curvilinear forms appear thanks to such architects as UN Studio or Greg Lynn.[36]

Charles Jencks recalled the deigns of Frank Gehry and Nicholas Grimshaw, as well as Peter Eisenman's, as the first examples of using computers to generate form in architecture which took on inspiration from mathematics and natural sciences.[37] Deconstructivism took inspiration from the philosophy of Jacques Derrida and the theory of catastrophe and chaos.[38] In this trend, an important role was played by factors connected both with the impact and the relations occurring between the components of the phenomena or design in question. For the philosopher of "architectural contemporaneity" Gilles Deleuze, an important aspect of culture was animation, based on constant change of factors which create a situation in time or space. Meaning, if we have "two" aspects of a certain situation, or in creating a thought about architecture, there is always a third condition – "an intermediate one." Animation can be used in shaping the architectural form. An example of this is the design of the Möbius House by UN Studio. On the design diagram in the shape of the Möbius strip, dependencies between the daily activities of inhabitants were shown. Creating a design in a digital environment was[39] a consequence of a previously developed diagram.

The Search for Contemporaneity

Seeking diversity is connected with the need of architects and investors to distinguish themselves or also results "out of boredom of the design's creator," as is noted by Dariusz Kozłowski:

> The recipient may be bored, but it is rather the impatience of the bored artist that is the driving force here. The times when the creator perfected his workshop for his entire life are a thing of the past. Today, nobody is surprised by the fact that the contemporary artist changes his creative approach numerous times during his path to perfection or more appropriately – the path which takes him on a search for the original.[40]

In this process, the drive to achieve perfection seems to be key, as Dutton would have us believe that, in a consumer society driven mainly by the media, the recognition of the product or company is of primary significance.[41] In architecture, the logo of the company often takes on the form of an icon – "a pattern." The task of an icon or a logo today is to replace a pattern which "has always been" a part of architecture. This is especially visible in public utility buildings or office buildings that became part of the brand of the city, region, or company.

The so-called *Bilbao Effect* can serve as an example. The irregular curvilinear body of the museum designed by Frank Gehry started a tourist boom in the city. The investment brought fame, which provided multimillion profits for the region.[42]

Another well-known example, also by Frank Gehry, is the DZ Bank Building in Berlin, 1995–2001, situated at Pariser Platz. The minimalist bank façade is made out of sandstone, while its modesty is underlined by the rhythm of the equally spaced windows. The interior is centered on the courtyard. Office spaces are located on three sides, while the fourth one serves a residential function. In the courtyard area, above the building there are curved glass roofs. The auditorium is centrally placed and is closed in a curvilinear form with dimensions of approximately 29 × 12 m and a height of about 10 m. The curves, which are a characteristic of Frank Gehry's architecture, were this time used in the interior of the facility.

In the second half of the twentieth century, it was not only fascination with modernity that was a source of new ideas in architecture. Aldo Rossi chose another path, namely, the sense of geometrical figures in architecture, which stemmed out of history. As Aldo Rossi put it:

> [A]rchitects should logically organize the geometrical elements of the design recalling memories and history of the place. Such architecture may

fit with the city, may continue its traditions, act as an invitation to passersby. Creating autonomous buildings in the urban space was a negation of the modernist ideals of Le Corbusier, which discarded history and created autonomous buildings in the city.[43]

Rossi himself created buildings out of raw stereometric bodies that referenced historical buildings; however, they had new implications. One of the most famous of his works is the San Cataldo Cemetery in Modena, 1971, which was inspired by nineteenth-century cemeteries.[44]

Aldo Rossi received the Pritzker Prize in 1990. In its verdict, the jury wrote:

> Rossi has been able to follow the lessons of classical architecture without copying them; his buildings carry echoes from the past in their use of forms that have a universal, haunting quality. His work is at once bold and ordinary, original without being novel, refreshingly simple in appearance but extremely complex in content and meaning. In a period of diverse styles and influences, Aldo Rossi has eschewed the fashionable and popular to create an architecture singularly his own.[45]

Rossi was an influential architect, while those who followed "the path of his thoughts," a way of simplified forms, included Giorgio Grassi (student halls of residence in Chieti, urban villa in Berlin), Mario Botta (Casa Rotonda), and Alberto Campo Baeza (the San Fermin Public School).[46]

Geometrical Haughtiness and New Materiality

Evolution and development in architecture, connected with the constant search for novelty and innovative technical, esthetic, and formal solutions, are a search connected with the need for prestige and social acceptance, which is provided to the architect by the crossing of borders of existing artistic, physical, and/or intellectual possibilities. These are most apparent in the features that we have named the geometrical haughtiness of form and new materiality, meaning, the use of atypical materials or use in a non-typical form. Numerous technical and designing limitations no longer exist; thus, complicated geometry in architecture turned out to be more accessible and often cheaper in use.

The architecture of the terminal in Madrid, 2005, by Richard Rogers takes advantage of the curvilinearity of form, but at the same time, there is a sense of an arrangement similar to those used in the initial concept of Saarinen's TWA terminal.

The interior of the Barajas Airport, despite its size, does not burden the user. This is due to the transparency of the body that merges the building with the Iberian landscape, but also thanks to the color scheme, which clearly separates the two departure halls of the Barajas terminal. Color is of dual significance; it livens the technological landscape of the interior and, at the same time, allows the traveler to ensure that he is in the appropriate location.[47] The materials used to finish off the covering of the great hall also alleviate the natural domination of technology over man, which is natural for an airport. Forming a building with oval "soft" shapes – moving away from a straight-line architectural structure – has become, to a large extent, or nearly completely dependent on, the imagination and the talent of the architect. Curvilinearity or geometrical exceptionality of form distinguishes the facility from the urban tissue, underlining the importance and function of the place. Good examples of this are the two New York–based facilities which refer to the shape of an ascending bird, the WTC Transportation Hub, 2016, by Santiago Calatrava,[48] and the New York by Gehry, 2005–2010, inspired by the sculptural form of Gian Lorenzo Bernini, which was earlier referred to as 8 Spruce Street.[49] Curvilinearity can be connected with the utility characteristic of the building. Such relations are visible in the case of stadiums, large concert halls, or entertainment arenas. In these facilities, curvilinearity influences conditions of visibility and acoustics. An appropriately shaped curvilinear form may also possess the desired utility and construction properties. For instance, the shape of the buildings of 30 St Mary Axe, 1997–2004, or the London City Hall, 1998–2002, by Foster & Partners is a result of the analysis of aerodynamics of form and the need to bring sunlight into the interior.[50] Architectural innovativeness often manifests itself in the search for solutions of contemporary, multi-layered materiality of the curtain walls.[51] It is visible in the buildings mentioned in this work, for example, the Cooper College, 2009, or office buildings such as the headquarters of the Hearst conglomerate in New York, 2006; the POLIN Museum of the History of Polish Jews in Warsaw, 2014; or the Center for the Meeting of Cultures in Lublin, 2015. Other examples of interest are industrial structures, where economic and utility requirements force the architect to use pragmatic spatial solutions. However, from time to time, to create a truly exceptional building which possesses the traits of an individually designed project, architects select technologically advanced construction materials, justifying it by the marketing function of the architecture of an industrial building.[52] The building of the warehouse of the Ricola Europe candy factory, 1993, in Mulhouse-Brunstatt in France, designed by Jacques Herzog and Pierre de Meuron, is simple in its form. It is characterized by a covering of semi-transparent polycarbonate panels decorated with an ornament with printed graphics and a plant motif. Dominique Perrault designed the factory and headquarters of the manufacturer of hook and loop fasteners Aplix in Le Cellier-sur-Loire, 1999. It is a rectangular building whose elevation is made up of steel panels with a mirror surface placed diagonally to each other. The surrounding landscape reflecting in the mirror-like surface creates an effect of unreality of the enormous monotonous structure. The 240 m long, relatively low building, thanks to the materials used in its elevation, on sunless days creates a form of a distinct character, while on other days, it merges into the surrounding sun-filled landscape. The warehouse and office building of the Tobias Grau company BRT Architekten, 1997–2007, boasts an unusual-for-industrial-architecture form of a flattened cylinder. The elevation is made up of mobile glass panels and photovoltaic cells. Both the form as well as the finishing materials of the building are to emphasize the modern, innovative character of the company and, as a result, the excellence of the manufactured product.[53] A trend of using a traditional material which was utilized in a formally innovative way is a continuation of the modernist search, which was abandoned in mass production. In literature, such an approach is referred to as "the new pleasure in materials."[54] The beauty of the stone wall is a distinguishing factor of the beauty of the Expo Pavilion in Barcelona, 1993, by Mies van der Rohe, presently the logo of the European Union Prize for Contemporary Architecture – the Mies van der Rohe Award.

Kengo Kuma, in a design of the headquarters of Louis Vuitton in Osaka, 2004, uses stone surfaces in the structure of the curtain walls of the elevation. However, this "contemporary stone" is not reminiscent of the traditional one. Created out of stone plates very thinly cut, it is semi-transparent, letting light into the interior of the building. In the evening, the stone plates create the beauty of the lit elevation, constituting the exceptionality and charm of the building.[55]

Herzog and De Meuron, in their Dominus Estate, 1986–1988, in California, built the simple body of the building out of gabions standing on top of each other. These walls, out of local stone, which "closed off" in a metal netting, play a double role – letting light in and, at the same time, protecting the interior from overheating. Such materiality of architecture places the building as part of the local landscape,[56] as a result elevating its value, as well as the price of the (sold) product.

The search for new materiality in architecture can be shown by presenting the elevations of buildings discussed in our work. We have selected examples that allow us to present the principal trends of new architectural materiality. These are:

- Traditionalism of material, at the present technique and/or technology, changes the formal image of the elevation, which still remains a matter from the historical record of usage of material. Such an example is stone willingly used by Alvaro Alto in "garden" architecture of the interwar period. The idea to "close off" the stone in a metal netting is still used today in the shape of gabions.[57] Ceramics used in contemporary architecture is not always reminiscent of brick; however, its formal otherness does not change the essence of the matter.
- Transparency and fleetingness of image in the contemporary search lead to a sensation of lightness and/or creating an illusion of weightlessness of

the building, and sometimes to the creation of a sensation of the unity of architecture with the surrounding landscape.
- The multi-layeredness of contemporary curtain walls helps in introducing "additional" functions to the external wall. Apart from the basic function of shielding the interior from outside conditions, the multi-layer curtain wall uses the diversity of the used materials in order to ensure the desired trait, for example, multimediality, transparency, energy savings.

The Ningbo History Museum, 2003–2008, by Wang Shu, was created in opposition to "contemporary, professional, soulless architecture." The idea of the architect was for the new museum to become "a town within a town," rooted in the history and identity of the place. During the construction of the reinforced concrete frame structure, old bricks, roof shingles, and stones from houses that were torn down in the area were used. The oldest elements are 1,500 years old. The placement of the old recovered material was planned; however, the arrangement of numerous fragments of the elevation could not have been predicted. The appearance of the elevation only became "obvious" when the bricklaying was finished.[58] Wang Shu received the Pritzker Prize in 2012 for

> producing an architecture that is timeless, deeply rooted in its context, and yet universal. . . . The History Museum at Ningbo is one of those unique buildings that while striking in photos, is even more moving when experienced. The museum is an urban icon, a well-tuned repository for history, and a setting where the visitor comes first. The richness of the spatial experience, both in the exterior and interior is remarkable. This building embodies strength, pragmatism, and emotion all in one.[59]

Idea, Design, Architect

The Design Process

The design process can be presented as a dialogue between a problem and its solution. Three components are important in said dialogue, namely:

- The thought – meaning, the design idea
- Designing the solution
- The architect – the designer

Thought and matter are the two principal elements in the creation of architecture – out of these two, thought is the basic material of architecture, although it is not quite architecture yet.[60] In the process of changing the "matter," the most important element is the design – presented in the form of a drawing or a model.

Computerization, which has also entered the production of construction elements, is more and more visible in the process of implementing architectural fantasies. But at the same time, the most important part of the architectural process is the thought, which is understood as the release of the creative imagination of the designer, the architect.[61]

In order to maintain a balance between the value of the designer's thought and contemporary possibilities of the computer, we may recall the words of Norman Foster:

> I have never had any objections to saying that which seems to be obvious, so it should come as no surprise when I suggest that, the pencil and the computer are if left to their own devices, equally dumb and only as good as the person driving them.[62]

Therefore, keeping in line with this, the process of shaping form in architecture begins with the shaping of the thought – the idea – by the designer, and this thought then can be developed in a digital environment. At the same time, models are becoming more and more relevant, especially during the initial phase of the designing process. Supported by an analysis of the pre-existing state, functionality, context of location, as well as the possibilities of modern technology of the planned structure, they become a more and more important element of the creation process.

A model allows for quicker access to conclusions on the subject of the effects of decisions made in the design. Jan Słyk justifies the value of modeling, recalling the words of Leon Batista Alberti contained in the second part of a book titled *On the Art of Building in Ten Books*. He quotes the author, who states that it is worth creating models "not to later regret what has been done."[63] It seems that modeling has become the basic value of digitalization for contemporary design in architecture. The ever-increasing range as well as the greater degree of dependencies in interdisciplinary connections in design have become a pretext for the creation and, later, for the universalization of pre-design research. *Research by design*[64] concerns a broadly understood process of analyses and studies that occur in the designing process, mainly at the stage of thoughts on the creating of form of the planned structure. This stage has always existed in architecture, but currently, in the process of creating the architectural work, as well as during a noticeable competitiveness of disciplines, it is becoming more and more important. Its basis in designing in architecture is:

- Maintaining the program and functional conditions as well as the spatial context
- Taking into account the existing, at a given time and place, technological possibilities

The popularization of the term *research by design* is, for the most part, due to the EAAE, the European Association for Architectural Education.[65] Independent of the level of usage of digital tools in the creation of the image of a future structure, it is still the idea that constitutes the principal thought, in which the architect creates design situations. Most often this initial thought is developed in the form of a sketch. Here it is worth repeating the words of Dariusz Kozłowski:

> The idea is created from start to finish in the brain, in a mysterious, not fully understood way. The beginning can be a pretext, which can take the shape of either a postcard or a crumb of history, as André Malraux noted in the Museum of Imagination, it can become a pretext for the creation of a form. In the past, during the Renaissance, a man was inscribed into the form of a square or a circle. He was the measure of excellence.[66]

Thought-sketches are quick and simple drawings for presenting the main thought of the author. The ability by the designer to impart a simple, intuitive concept is especially important in the initial phase of design creation – in the creation/formation phase of the idea of the structure. In showing the principal thought of the architect, it generally leads to the implementation of the work. More and more frequently, the designed structure, almost since its inception, is created as a three-dimensional computer model. However, this does not have a great influence on the decrease of the significance of the idea in creating architectural concepts. One can even say that the idea-thought still plays a key role in the quality of the investment. Then, the thought shown in the drawing-sketch creates a balance between the dream of the creator and the depiction of this dream in the process of erecting the structure, allowing for a "painless" passage from dream to a new reality. The image of the city on the drawing by the young Sant Elia from early modernism today creates the possibility of checking how dreams on the perception of future form in architecture, expressed in the drawing-dream. Currently, it is of utmost importance to recall the "idea of urban density," which, in a nearly perfect way, is expressed in the sketch by Zaha Hadid. The drawing, depicting the idea of urban density, shows a concept of competition for the building of the *Peak Hong-Kong* club from the eighties of the twentieth century. This passage in time and space is symbolic.

The architect-designer, who can use knowledge taken from professional experience, possesses theoretical knowledge, and can use creative reflection, always boasts a close relationship with the time and place in which the structure is created. Therefore, independent of the pragmatics of the creation of the work, or the avant-garde aspirations of the designer, the reality of the area in which the building is created always leaves its mark on the form and estheticism of the structure. In the act of the creation of the structure, the designer-architect struggles with the matter, similarly to an artist creating a painting or a sculpture. Similarly to a manager of a large corporation, he must rapidly react to the dreams of contemporaneity, but also its technical and technological capabilities. The source of dreams is most often patterns – for architecture, patterns have always been important. Today, when everything seems possible, more and more patterns are narrowed. The set of structures that had previously seemed impossible to construct is also shrinking. However, if we notice that, thanks to access to computer technology, the architect "is able to do more," it frequently means that the recipient must also learn to comprehend new architectural reality.

In the past, patterns were made and also transported to various parts of the world by specialized groups of wandering carpenters and masons. Today, patterns are presented in books, and we become familiar with them through various kinds of media. Dreams and thoughts are transported to various places, and often, this requires correction or rethinking and even the intervention into the dream. Prizes of particular significance are those that distinguish the architectural structures due to certain particular features. Such an award in architecture is the annual Pritzker Prize. It makes the public aware of the architectural values of the awarded structure. Therefore, in the entire designing process, the architect plays a key role and must be able to compare but also take advantage of the experiences of others. This ability, known as *knowing-in-action* and *reflection-in-action*, is specific knowledge, important for the effectiveness in designing in architecture, but also in related engineering fields.[67]

For the creation of the new structure, the efficiency of the designer is very important. We can speak of a specific ability, of creative passion, which is granted to some of us "since the beginning," when others are forced to toil for many years in order to improve it. This ability is not bestowed upon everybody in equal shares. It is usually referred to as talent.

At the conclusion of these reflections, let us recall the Sendai Mediatheque by Toyo Ito & Associates, 1995–2000. Shaped in the form of a seven-story cuboidal glazed box, it boasts fluid connections between stories. They are created by posts constructed in the form of spatial tubes. The construction of the form of the poles creates this sensation of the connection between levels. In order to compare the building with the thought of the designer, we can see a *magnificent* lapidary in drawing sketch of the cross section showing the finesse of the thought of the architect, who speaks of architecture as if of a "dress thrown on top of it."[68]

Architects – The Creators Speak with Their Own Words

The statements made by architects-creators should probably be taken into account when writing on the subject of the creation of form in architecture. An example that seems to connect the seventies of the twentieth century with contemporary expressionism is the work of Hans Hollein. In presenting the small candle shop designed by Hollein, situated in an exclusive shopping street in the center of Vienna, it is worth recalling a statement by the author, who says "we build what we want, creating architecture, which is not determined by technology, but one that uses this technology – pure, absolute architecture."[69]

22 The Continuity of Thought in Architecture

Helmut Jahn,[70] the author of over 100 structures, has this to say when it comes to architecture:

> When I am given a task of designing a building, I must analyze all its aspects. I don't always try and create something new. I rather take from the past and try to improve on it. I take advantage of new methods, improve the technology, correct the parameters, which had become important in the meantime, e.g. energy-efficiency of the building. . . . Archi-neering is an approach, in which the architect very closely cooperates with the engineer almost from the onset of the design, and as a result, every element of the building works better than if traditional methods had been used. Currently, it has become a rule, that a building can only gain when modern technological solutions are used in it, but the architect cannot deal with it himself. That is why so many subcontractors take part in the creation process.[71]

Dariusz Kozłowski,[72] architect and a laureate of the honorary SARP Award in 2011, the creator, along with Wacław Stefański and Maria Misiągiewicz, of the Higher Theological Seminary of the Resurrectionist Congregation in Cracow, says that "ever since beauty has departed along with classical art, architects were left with only the search for originality."[73] This is what he thinks of architecture, but he prefers to talk about the opera: "I believe that opera is the

Figure 1.1 Casa Olajossy ossia Villa in Fortezza. A single-family house by Dariusz Kozłowski and Tomasz Kozłowski, Lublin, 2011.

Source: From the archive of Dariusz Kozłowski.

most refined type of art, the most artificial of all the arts, this great lie, which consists of literature, sculpture, architecture, painting."[74] And about studies:

> Students have too many classes. . . . The time for reflection does not come until their diploma work. . . . [E]ven a university cannot stop those who want to become architects. . . . If someone is to be a great architect, creating original things, he must be a rebel, negate everything that surrounds him. He can choose some Classicist to be his master, e.g. Le Corbusier.[75]

He further goes on to say:

> Architecture appears when we go further than simple usefulness would require. Ever since beauty has departed along with classical art, architects were left with only the search for originality. For instance, my students choose an image for their diploma work, most often constructivist abstraction, they search for a place for it on the city plan. Then they transfer this flat image into a spatial thing, axonometry, perspective drawing. In the end, functional solutions can be introduced into this uncovered figure. This is an uncovering of forms liberated from the dictate of functions, shapes, which are already embedded in the city.[76]

Figure 1.2 A sketch of the Agora building in Warsaw, JEMS architects, 2002.
Source: Maciej Miłobędzki/JEMS Architekci.

24 The Continuity of Thought in Architecture

JEMS Architekci,[77] the creators of numerous beautiful buildings, speak thusly about their credo:

> We are joined by a conviction that, reading of culture, history, tradition, the context of a place, human needs, constitutes the condition and foundation of creating culture. We treat reality both as a matter used for creation as well as the framework of our activity. . . . [A]lso in limitations and conflicts that contemporaneity brings with it, we search for the source of inspiration. We traverse areas, that often do not provide us with the opportunity to create quick unambiguity and a synthetic design response. We have never dreamed of a universal method – a strategy.
>
> The observations, images, associations, sensations, and rules and regulations found in the course of our studies, we discover "along the way" driven by the experience and intuition gained over the years. New discoveries that surprise even ourselves emerge on our path. They provide meaning to our efforts. In our works, we attempt to find that which is specific for individual topics. We try to define the topic so that it would come to be. . . . [W]e search not only for the essence of things but for the things themselves. We refer to that which is beyond-historical, order, tectonics, fascination with the natural abilities of materials, light, passing

Figure 1.3 A sketch of the extension of the Birthplace of Fryderyk Chopin and Park in Żelazowa Wola by Bolesław Stelmach, Żelazowa Wola, 2010.

Source: Bolesław Stelmach/Stelmach & Partners Architectural Office.

time, proportions, and principles of form construction. We have derived the most satisfaction from designs, which were created as cohesive, whole notions.[78]

Bolesław Stelmach,[79] an architect, has this to say about the Chopin Museum in Żelazowa Wola:

I simply solve civil engineering problems, search for a rational, least expensive, and best-functioning structure. I do something that is very easy: a function enclosure built out of stone, wood, and glass. The Russian director Andrei Tarkovsky said, that realistic art is an art that shows the truth. In architecture, there exists a truth of structure and function. In my buildings one can see the rhythm of supports made out of glued timber as a rhythm of trees in a park, installations run on the construction, there is not even a sliver of plaster, which would cover up anything. . . . I act, according to the advice of the Japanese architect Kengo Kuma – I search for conditions to create a structure in place. I sit down and observe what possesses value in the area, how the light falls, where the wind blows from. That is why there is so much glass in my buildings.[80]

Tomasz Konior,[81] an architect who loves music, says:

At the Faculty of Architecture in Cracow, I was taught sensitivity to architecture. . . . A strong, industrial context, the golden age for Silesia, meaning the twenties of the previous century, is what today creates the foundation of the "Silesian School" Architects and architecture were shaped by this context, that teaches to think reasonably, pragmatically, and rationally approach the design process. . . . It is here that I hear that "function is beauty" and it seems that over those several years I was filled with such thinking. . . . Since childhood, I have been fascinated with the construction site. This possesses a metaphysical dimension. . . . The idea and the design

Figure 1.4 Sketches of the State Music School No. 1 in Warsaw, Tomasz Konior, 2015.

Source: Tomasz Konior/Konior Studio.

are already in place, yet the architecture is still missing. Construction is the decisive stage for a building. . . . [T]he confrontation of idea with reality is sometimes difficult. Either the standard and a ready system, or a "wild ride" and the search for methods to reach the destination. Satisfaction comes when we succeed. There are times when we must admit defeat and try to repair, that which has been damaged. This is what the adventure with architecture is all about, it comes to life through the work of many people and various talents. In reality, we are not the sole authors of the work. We are the creators of an idea.[82]

Marek Budzyński,[83] an architect individualist, the creator of clearly distinguishable works, when he was faced with the question of whether Polish architecture can be beautiful, said, "When Michelangelo was asked how to obtain a work of art he responded: it must be entrusted to a master. That is the only response I can give."[84]

Discourse on Architectural Space

The Creation of Architectural Form

The question on the creation of architectural form, which has always intrigued, still seems valid. In design theories, one can find concepts that can provide a basis for ordering the questions about the emergence of form in architecture. For the assumption presented in the introduction, the theory of beauty by G. Hans Gadamer[85] is of significance. This theory minimizes the importance of social and political factors while distinguishing beauty as the principal trigger in shaping architecture. In the discussion on the history of the Western theory of design, Mark Gelernter[86] lists five principal trends, five ideas, or five concepts that may constitute the foundation for classifying discussions on the creation of form in architecture. These are:

- *Function shapes the architectural form* of the planned building. Per this concept, the form mainly corresponds to the needs of the investor or/and user. Examples of such buildings are a stadium, concert hall, etc., for which visibility or proper acoustics are generally the principal distinguishing feature in the search for formal solutions. However, among such structures, there are solutions which are formally different, although they were created in similar place or time.
- *Architectural form is generated by the creative imagination* of the creator. The form of the structure is, above all, the effect of intuition, knowledge, and sensitivity of the architect-designer. However, even the work of a very talented team can result in solutions that do not correspond to the accepted principles of quality of architecture. This generally takes place as a result of a sudden "financial crash" or unexpected localization difficulties.[87]

- *Architectural form is created as a result of the impact of the so-called spirit of the age on the place.* It does not matter just how much of his own vision of architecture a designer has; generally, he is tied down by the views and opinions of the community in which he lives and works. The author (MG) invokes buildings created in a similar time period: the Bauhaus building in Dessau (W. Gropius, 1926), the Viceroy's House (now Rashtrapati Bhavan) in New Delhi in India (Sir E. Lutyens, 1911–1931).
- *Architectural form is, to a large extent, determined by the pre-existing economic and social conditions.* They enable or hinder the actions of the architect. However, if in the first case they are a result of the want to change the traditional way of thinking and the drive towards formal solutions resulting from imagination and the desire to change the existing stereotype, in case of dependence on the existing social or economic conditions, imagination is limited. Generally, this is a process that is parallel to the limiting of the creative possibilities and aspirations of the architect.
- *Architectural form stems from timeless formal laws.* This theory emphasizes the fact that certain forms in architecture are universal, for example, basilica, atrium, courtyard. Repeated in numerous solutions, they become the basis of a general concept, independent of the designing assumptions, independent of culture, time, and place. Detailed solutions may vary and transform to a certain degree. However, generally, the formal connection is clearly visible.[88]

Ecstatic Architecture

Each year, in the late autumn, in Cracow, meetings of architects take place, with the aim to discuss architecture. Each year the topic of discussion is different, but it is connected by the problem of defining architectural space. In 2015, the organizers decided to reward the most faithful participants with a medal. The drawing of a unicorn here appears in a circular field on a metal badge. Legends say that wherever a unicorn appears, the place becomes important and man can fulfill his dreams. The appearance in the text of a unicorn, a mysterious and legendary creature, brings us closer to architecture, because in architecture there is a mystery of the creation of thought – an image of the future structure. But there is also knowledge about matter and construction. For the building to be created, we need enthusiasm and determination. And then there are costs. As is calculated by some, contemporary architecture is, apart from perhaps wars and space programs, the most expensive activity of the current society.[89] Despite these ever-growing costs, we still create architecture so that it may surround us, so that we may safely lock away our lives inside and develop our dreams. Finally, it seems that creating our own surroundings is, after all, a greater priority than creating programs about extraterrestrial beings.

28 The Continuity of Thought in Architecture

In 1997, in the *Royal Academy of Arts* in London, the critic of architecture Charles Jencks conducted a debate on the topic of contemporary architecture. The result of the 48-hour debate was the term "ecstatic" architecture to describe architecture that expresses emotionality and expression of form.[90]

The sixteenth-century sculpture *The Ecstasy of Saint Theresa* by Gian Lorenzo Bernini from the Church of Santa Maria della Vittoria in Rome became the symbol of such architectural sensitivity. The most important characteristic of a structure with such architecture is the sensation of movement and dematerialization of form. These features are noticeable in the works of contemporary architecture. The architect and architecture theoretician Neil Leach noticed the irony in the fact that it was the sculpture of Bernini that was granted such unbelievable, timeless applause and not the structure of one of the great builders of the Baroque period.[91]

The debate, and especially the distinguishing of the sculpture of St. Theresa, leads us to a reflection on the versatility of the talent of the architect, but also to emphasize a theme, where the utility of the created building becomes more important than its architectural form.

In what follows, we recall two illustrations, out of which one shows *The Ecstasy of St. Theresa*, the famous sculpture of Bernini, which became the symbol of an inspired, emotional thought of the architect. The other depicts a skyscraper in New York which houses the Hearst company, which we have selected as a presentation and image of a pragmatic thought of a contemporary architect – Sir Norman Foster.

Ecstatic architecture can be compared to the expressionism of early modernism. Its contemporary form moves towards a trend of lightness and fleetingness of formal as well as material solutions. This architectural "fleetingness" is especially clearly visible in the landscape of contemporary cities. The use of various technological capabilities of glass strengthens the sensation of "non-materiality" of the urban landscape. Architecture, in broadening its relations with science, more than willingly uses the effects of technical solutions that have their source in biotechnology and informatization.

The participants in the London Royal Academy of Arts noticed that frequently, at the time when we first come into contact with contemporary innovativeness in architecture, an ecstatic form may cause us to feel surprised, even shocked.[92] Around us, often without being noticed, houses with amazing shapes are being built, while the landscape of cities and towns of the first part of the new century has rapidly begun to change.

In 2017, the book *The Age of Spectacle: Adventures in Architecture and the 21st-Century City* was published in London.[93] The author, Tom Dyckhoff, begins with a question: "Why did the British build big pants for the Chinese?"[94] He referred to architecture with surprising geometry in a much less subtle way than did the participants in the London Royal Academy discussion, but definitely unambiguously – namely, Wowhaus. Here is what Dyckhoff writes about it:

> [W]hen as an architectural critic for "The Times" . . . I sat across from John Prescott, at that time deputy to Tony Blair – as he was the politician responsible for spatial planning – the most influential man in the world of British architecture, who said "people ask me what does the word wow mean?" . . . Take a look. Here it is. We have defined it by combining architects, urban planners, and developers in one common action – we have created the new wow factor – THIS IS WHAT WOW IS! These are buildings which are stunning.[95]

When we think of the various needs and trends of the creation of architecture shown here, it seems that the sensation of the dematerialization of form, along with the wow effect, is not the expression of the opposition of thought but more concerns the diversity of formal solutions. It is an expression of the innovativeness of contemporary architecture.

"Wowhouse"[96]

If we look at the architecture of recent years, those that draw our attention – surprise us – are buildings that seemingly are compact, simple in form, while the mystery of the amazement – the architectural WOW – is hidden in the interior structure of the building. We would like to present this thought using three examples; these are the university building known as Cooper Union in New York, 2009; the POLIN Museum of History of Polish Jews in Warsaw, 2013; and the NOSPR building in Katowice, 2014.

COOPER UNION IN NEW YORK, 2009

ARCHITECTURE:	Morphosis, Thom Mayne
Floor Space:	16,300 m²
Investment Cost:	166 million USD
Design:	2004
Completion:	2009

The Cooper Union university building, by Thom Mayne, *Morphosis*, 2009, is an extension of the university complex Cooper Union College. The genesis of the school is similar to that of the London-based AA. Still today it remains a small school, with many applicants and few open places, while its graduates include numerous well-known architects.[97]

The idea of Thom Mayne, an architect from the Morphosis group, was to create a place that would serve as an intellectual "link" between the cultural and the technical community of the university and their surroundings, meaning, the residential district of Lower Manhattan. As a result, the architect, a recipient of the Pritzker Prize in 2005 as well as the AIA Gold Medal in 2013, created a structure on Manhattan that is more reminiscent of an extravagant sculpture than a building. The unusual, seemingly unstable form of the building, as if to counterbalance it, is supported by large poles in the shape of the letter *V* from the entrance. However, the geometry of form is not the only thing that makes the structure stand out from its surroundings. The architectural shape of the building seems to directly respond to the contemporary need for otherness. The external covering of the structure looks like a "ripped" outer "skin," strengthening the expression of the architectural form. Despite this sensation, the drawing of the plan is cohesive and orderly. And even more surprisingly, the building, which is located within the frontage of the street, does not shock the surrounding area with its form. In a photograph from the construction period (2006–2007), we can see a nine-story hexagon with orthogonal divisions of the interior. The only extravagant part of the ruled structure in the internal patio opened up through the full height of the building. The area around the patio consists of the school's open spaces: galleries, auditoriums, as well as the main staircase that connects the first, fifth, and eighth floor in the so-called skip-and-stop system. The top floor is closed off with a terrace and a green roof. The effectively constructed staircase plays the role of the principal architectural "amazement" or the aforementioned WOW of the structure. The architectural beauty of the building is, to a large extent, an effect of the cladding – semi-transparent, double "skin" of the facility which surrounds the functional and constructional structure of the body. The shape and the material form of the cladding create the sculpting of the structure, reinforcing the feeling of expression. The external panels of the cladding – multi-layered, made of glass and aluminum – allow for transparency of locations important for the functionality of the interior, while also ensuring usability comfort. In the summer, they reduce heating of the interior, while in the winter, they ensure access to sunlight. Cooper Union, despite its non-standard architectural beauty, appears to be located in the appropriate place. The calm, bourgeois character of the district creates a nearly perfect academic surroundings, to which the body of the college is an excellent supplement.[98]

THE POLIN MUSEUM OF THE HISTORY OF POLISH JEWS IN WARSAW, 2013

ARCHITECTURE:	Mahlamäki and Lahdelma Architects
Floor Space:	16,000 m²
Investment Cost:	320 million PLN
Design:	2005–2008
Completion:	2009–2013

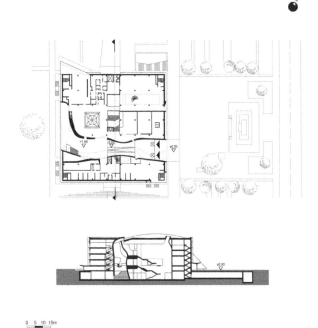

Figure 1.5 The POLIN Museum of the History of Polish Jews, floor plan and section.
Source: Filip Zamiatnin/book authors.

The POLIN Museum of the History of Polish Jews by Rainer Mahlamäki and Ilmari Lahdelma (2013) is situated in Muranów, near the Ghetto Heroes Monument. The aim of the structure was not to be a reminder of the Holocaust. Its function is twofold; it is to tell of the input of the Jewish nation into the history of Poland and to become a cultural and educational center. The building was created in stages: in 1998, a decision of the concept of the building was reached; in 2005, a competition took place, which 245 architects entered; and finally, out of 119 applications, the international jury invited 11 teams to present their concept of the museum. The victors were Lahdelma and Mahlamäki from Finland. The building received first prize in an online plebiscite organized in 2014, the Architecture Award in Chicago, and the Design of the Year Award of the SARP (Association of Polish Architects) in 2013.

The building itself boasts four stories aboveground and two underground. Thanks to geometrical simplicity and height, which seamlessly blend into the surroundings – the residential buildings, which were created in the post-war years, in the rebuilt Polish capital – the building fits nearly perfectly in this location. An important trait of the museum building is the architectural simplicity of form. It hides its symbolism in specific features, in details; however, this symbolism is overbearing neither towards the passer-by nor the visitor.

This great architectural "box" on the plan of a square has its "WOW effect" hidden inside the pragmatically shaped body. The keystone of the interior is the entrance hall. In its architectural shape, the history of the Jewish nation is hidden. It can be understood in two separate ways, as a recalling of the Crossing of the Red Sea or as a discontinuation of the history of Polish Jews during the Holocaust. The sensation of a "tearing" of the building, all the way to the height of the covering, created a high passage, which is clearly visible in the interior. This passage, in the shape of a ravine, with irregularly undulating walls, covered with shotcrete, runs across the structure of the building, finishing off with a light that flows through from outside the external wall of the building. Looking on from the outside, the building is reminiscent of an enormous glass display case filled to the brim with books of the Torah. The glass panels that make up the cladding have the name POLIN (POLAND) inscribed within. Thanks to the simplicity of form and elegance of the façade, the architecture of the building is moving, indeed.

Figure 1.6 The POLIN Museum of the History of Polish Jews by Mahlamäki and Lahdelma Architects.

Source: Tomasz Kubaczyk.

POLISH NATIONAL RADIO SYMPHONY ORCHESTRA IN KATOWICE, 2013

ARCHITECTURE:	Tomasz Konior, Konior Studio
Floor Space:	35,059.5 m^2
Investment Cost:	320 million PLN
Design:	2008–2012
Completion:	2012–2043

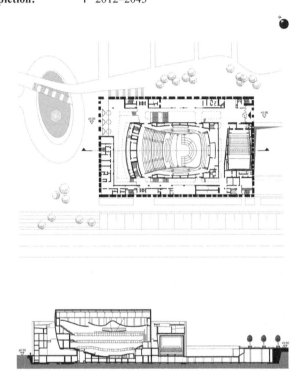

Figure 1.7 Polish National Radio Symphony Orchestra, floor plan and section.

Source: Filip Zamiatnin/book authors.

The NOSPR in Katowice, by Tomasz Konior, 2014, houses the Polish National Radio Symphony Orchestra. It is situated in Katowice, the capital city of the largest industrial region in Poland, in which a former industrial zone has been replaced by the Katowice Culture Zone. The NOSPR building is one of the first elements of the Zone. The competition, announced in 2008, was won by Tomasz Konior, an architect who had previously completed another widely acclaimed "musical building" in Katowice – the Symfonia Concert Hall.

The NOSPR building was created on the premises of a former woodyard of a shut down minc near the buildings of the university as well as the famous

Silesian Spodek (1971). The building neighbors the glass cubicles of the newly established museum as well as the building of the International Congress Center, which closes off the area, which was named Silesian Acropolis by the well-known Polish architect Stanisław Niemczyk.[99] The famous NOSPR concert hall, hidden inside a concentrically formed plan, is barely visible from the outside.[100] The architecture, showing the repetitiveness of brick pilasters, brings to mind thoughts of a keyboard, although the author himself refers to it as "Silesian chimneys."

The building, formed according to the principles of right-angle geometry, only very slightly suggests that inside – like the "Silesian pearl in the crown"[101] – it hides a great concert hall with 1,800 seats. The rooms accompanying the hall emphasize the centripetal concept of the plan. They are the second, outer ring of rooms, which surround the great hall, around the external walls of the building. This external ring contains a bookshop, a restaurant, as well as a second smaller chamber hall for 300 people. Both the small and large concert halls have external wood finishing.

The space in the large hall is shaped similarly to the hall of the Scharoun Philharmonic in Berlin. The stage, partly surrounded by the audience, brings the listeners closer to the musicians. The dark, slightly bent surfaces of the audience walls emphasize the oval drawing of the plan. The interior causes the listener to feel as if he were inside a magical circle filled to the brim with music. The architectural beauty of the NOSPR concert hall is supplemented by good visibility conditions and the oft-underlined excellent acoustics of the interior of the concert hall, which is the WOW effect of the NOSPR building.

The NOSPR building has received numerous prizes and distinctions, out of which the most important one is being part of the ECHO (European Concert Hall Organization),[102] which brings together the best concert halls in Europe.

Figure 1.8 Polish National Radio Symphony Orchestra, by Tomasz Konior, Konior Studio, 2014.

Source: Bartek Barczyk/Konior Studio.

Rationalism or Emotions

Looking on at the three buildings described previously, we may try to find the response to the question, What is more important for the thought of the architect-designer – emotion and intuition of the creator or the rationality of the creative search? This question is difficult, similar to the questions that may be encountered in the content of Shakespearean dramas: What is more important in the life of the Shakespearean heroine, "beauty or brains"? This question is akin to the question we would like to ask the creator of architectural work. The answer is also comparable; each of the two mentioned characteristics is an equally important trait of the designer-architect.

In wanting to further analyze the subject, it is important that the aforementioned buildings with a structure of a "right-angle geometry" "hide" a surprise inside – an autonomous architectural element of curvilinear geometry.

In contemporary architecture, curvilinearity of the building structure generally results in a solution that is technically more advanced or a selection of solutions that sharply raise the costs of the investment. Even though there is not enough research done on this subject,[103] deciding on the curvilinearity of the structure is generally associated with an emotional character of the designer-creator, or with the way a solution was chosen. However, we may say that buildings in which the rationality of structure of right-angle geometry occurs together with a curvilinearity of solutions that are a surprise to the user/ observer result in an architecturally exceptional building. To support this, we can quote Antonio Gaudi, who said, "The straight line belongs to man. The curved one to God."[104]

The three aforementioned examples generally depict formally harmonious solutions, with a "predictable" character of the interior. In each of them, we find this so-called unexpected architectural amazement, which strengthens the sensation of the exceptionality of the structure.

In the 41 Cooper Square university building, such a WOW effect is the internal patio with the main staircase, with a structure that is completely different from the rest of the building. The elegant, balanced structure of the building of the POLIN museum contrasts and amazes with the interior of the entry hall. The enclosing of this fragment of the building within the softness of the walls is simply amazing, and it is distinguishable from the straight-line structure of the remaining interiors of the building.

In both buildings, the architect, creator, and designer transferred the contemporary need for innovativeness and formal searches, which are an expression of the *zeitgeist* and the *genius loci*. If we would like to classify the NOSPR architecture in accordance with the concepts described by M. Gelernter, we could say that the oval plan of the audience "has always been" a part of Western culture. On the other hand, the finesse and culture of the design solutions are the doing of the knowledge, intuition, and talent of the designer-architect. The so-called *architectural WOW effect* is the beauty of the curvilinearity of the concert hall supported by its exceptional acoustics.

Figure 1.9 The grand concert hall of the Polish National Radio Symphony Orchestra, by Tomasz Konior, Konior Studio, 2014.

Source: Daniel Rumiancew/Konior Studio.

Diversity and Surprise

On Creativity

Architecture seems to be a simple matter – "four walls and a roof," says Reiner de Graaf, who immediately after this subtitle adds: "the complex nature of a simple profession."[105] He expressed perhaps the most important characteristic of contemporary architecture. All actions connected with creating, meaning, designing, and then with the implementation of architecture are becoming more and more complex, requiring the participation of many professions, not only the payment of bills, but also the collaboration of numerous minds. As a result, the architect becomes the author of an idea,[106] the principal thought which accompanies the creation of the work from its inception until its completion. Generally, in the process of the creation of a structure, the idea is when we first see otherness, a new quality of the building. It is also a reflection of the creativity of the architect, the creator of the design.

Creativity is the property of our mind – our imagination to create new, surprising, and valuable things. The term itself, rather ambiguous, can be understood in various ways. Pablo Picasso says that "the greatest enemy of creativity is common sense." However, Marcus du Sautoy, in recalling the hours spent on pondering and recording calculations and, finally, remembering the moment of finding a solution, says, "That sheer buzz of excitement is the allure of creativity."[107]

Creativity is present in very simple, everyday activities; it is not reserved exclusively for art. Limiting ourselves to art, a field that is close to architecture, seems to provide appropriate but also sufficient material for comparison. Invoking once again the book by Marcus du Sautoy *The Creativity Code*, we may quote Margaret Boden, a specialist on cognitive psychology, who identifies three variations of human creativity:[108]

- *Exploratory creativity*, which is based on expanding the borders of the existing principles and rules. The author provides an example, where the music of Bach constitutes the peak at which the musicians of the Baroque studied tonality. Its preludes and fugues were the border which was finally crossed by the music of Mozart and Beethoven.[109]
- *Combinational creativity* is based on the combination of the principles of one field to create new patterns for creators of a *different world* of values. And thus Zaha Hadid combined the love of pure forms of the painter Kazimierz Malewicz with her knowledge of architecture to create a unique style of rounded buildings.[110]
- *Transformational creativity*, distinguished by Boden, is the most fleeting. As an example, she gives Picasso's cubism or Schoenberg's atonality. Transformational changes are often based on the changes in the rules of

the game, or they require the rejection of the guidelines accepted by the previous generation and the creation of new principles. For instance, the romantic trend in music is connected with a whole slew of violations of the rules. Schumann left unsolved accords which both Haydn and Mozart would have felt obliged to supplement.[111]

The creativity of each trend can be evaluated in comparison with the previous period. Therefore, creativity is not an absolute action but a relative one. We are creative within the confines of our culture and a specific system of reference.[112]

The three examples of the architecture shown in the following were put in the book prior to adding the short description on creativity. For us they became even more important after becoming familiar with the content of the quoted book, since they allowed us to include creativity in architecture among the creators in other fields, including art. "The Creativity Code" as well as the fascination with the selection of our examples which correspond to the three types/kinds of creativities distinguished by Boden were the reason for expanding the text. And so:

- Thermal Baths in Vals are an example of the broadening of rules for a more distinct depiction of the contemporarily existing borders in shaping the image of architecture, meaning, exploratory creativity.
- The architecture of the Rolex Learning Center shows the use of a combination of principles of geometry to create a new image of architectural space – meaning, the use of combinational creativity.
- The architecture of the Paris Philharmonic is a private attempt to reject numerous rules and create new ones for the beauty of the architectural image of the building – it is an expression of transformational creativity.

In contemporary architecture, we can see the plurality and diversity of approaches to expressing the creator's own architectural imagination and creativity. The relations seen earlier are visible in world examples, out of which three we would like to present: the Thermal Baths in Vals in Switzerland, the Rolex Learning Center in Lausanne, and the Paris Philharmonic. These examples all possess the features of the contemporary searches as far as the diversity of formal concepts, creativity, and surprise.

Thermal Baths in Vals, 1996, arch. Peter Zumthor, are situated on the slope of a mountain, and they are a reference to the surrounding landscape. The interior consists of small intimate rooms for bathing which are finished off in stone. The rawness of the building material, well-thought-out lighting, as well as water creates an atmosphere of peace and beauty. The choice of stone was very important for Peter Zumthor, both for the idea of the design, the thoughts of the concept, as well as the further decision-making process.

Stone in Zumthor's architecture is more than a simple utility – it has, since the beginning, been a thought that was the basis of the idea of the designer. "The most important was to create the place – a modest building, connected with the local culture."[113] The context, idea, and content were of primary significance to the architect in this design. The author himself writes: "Mountain, stone, water – building in the stone, building with the stone, building into the mountain, building out of the mountain, being inside the mountain – that is how we can interpret the implications and the sensuality of associating these words, architecturally."[114] Looking at the image of the building, *inserted* into the slope of a mountain, it seems that it brings us closer to silence which exists in the image of La Tourette to the thoughts of Corbu – the old master of modernism.

The Rolex Learning Center in Lausanne, 2010, arch. SANAA Design Studios, shows an interesting approach to the solutions of the spatial arrangement. As a result, the drawing of the plan shows an almost-rectangular building; however, the distinct curvature of the ceilings, which defines the interior, causes the entire building to express a "softness" of form.[115] The whole is a uniform construction, which is in part bent, while in part it "lies" flatly on the ground. The bent part of the structure floats in a way that allows for the placement of public space below the level of the building and also for the placement of the main entrance to the building in the center of the elongated-in-form plan.

Apart from a library, the building also includes exhibition spaces, lecture halls, conference halls, workshops for students and academics, offices, cafés, restaurants, and places to relax.[116] All functions are placed on one undulating surface. Inside, there are no clear borders between each of the zones. Instead of stairs, delicate ramps and terraces were used. Besides rooms for various forms of group activities, the building also includes spaces for quiet, individual work. They are acoustically isolated through the changes in height of the building. In addition, spaces for group activities were also designed, divided by glass walls. There are 14 atriums in the building with various curvilinear shapes and various sizes.

All the outside walls are covered in glass, which allows for more light in the broad interior. The rooms located at higher levels boast a view of the lake and the Alps. It provides the possibility to create visual relations between the interior and exterior of the building. The Rolex Center surprises with its creativity in the creation of curvilinear form, which has caused the building to become a trademark of both Switzerland and the Swiss Federal Institute of Technology in Lausanne.[117]

The Paris Philharmonic building, 2007–2015, arch. Jean Nouvel, conforms to the concept of geometrical complexity and curvilinearity. The building is situated in the neighborhood of distinct postmodern and deconstructive structures.[118] The building neighbors the Parc de la Villette on the outskirts of Paris. Jean Nouvel, in winning the competition, proposed a very distinct form. The Paris Philharmonic is, therefore, a building with complicated geometry and equally as complicated materiality. The roof is a generally accessible public space with a view of the panorama of Paris. Visually, the Philharmonic building consists of a shining body with a spiral form, which contrasts with the angular, matted cladding. It is created by a mosaic made of metal panels, which are reminiscent of the shapes of birds. This form utilized by Jean Nouvel is a continuation of the ideas that shape nearby structures. The concert hall for 2,400 listeners – *la Grande Salle Pierre Boulez* – is acoustically perfect. Thanks to the fact that it possesses technical equipment aided with movable elements, the audience can accommodate up to 3,500 people. For the architect Jean Nouvel, the formal search for "otherness" in the architecture of a building is a continuation of trends that were started in nearby structures and the park. As he himself explains, "[t]he Paris Philharmonic exists as a prestigious event, which maintains harmonious relations with the Parc de la Villette, La Cité de la Musique, and the Paris beltway."[119] The enormous dimensions and complicated geometry turn this more into intellectual musings than actual "harmonious" incorporation of the philharmonic into the urban context.

The three buildings, of which each shows a different idea, are surprisingly different in the formal expression; each serves a different function. Despite differences in the creative approaches of architects, each building is the expression of the creativity of its author. It is also an expression of the drive for architectural perfection and the desire to quench human dreams and desires.

Concept, Context, Content

The architectural idea often precedes the introduction of the content of the functional program. However, it is the function, meaning, the content included in the architectural form, that confirms the value of the structure, underlines Bernard Tschumi.

Many examples of modernist architecture show that the concept of the building can match the program and content to a lesser or greater degree.[120] Yet the architecture is always created in the context of its surroundings. We are reminded of this by Bernard Tschumi,[121] who says that a structure always exists in specific surroundings – in a geographic location, in a context that is historically, culturally, and economically defined.

The concept which influences the form of the building can have various connections with the context. In describing the importance of the context, Tschumi introduces three relations into the discussion which are possible in the relations between concept and context.

- *Indifference* means the independence of the concept from the context. The context of the structure and its architectural idea coexist independently in space and do not interact with each other. Frequently, when the idea is formulated in such a way, it is the beginning of a new identity of a place.

- *Mutuality* occurs when the idea of the architect for the structure and its location supplement each other, often in such a way that it seems they constitute one whole and the change from one to the other is almost unnoticeable.
- *Conflict* assumes the need to develop and consensus between the form of the structure and its context.[122]

The relations between the architectural concept and context presented earlier allow for simultaneous consideration of the location context and the cultural context, while architects can choose from at least three approaches to the relation of idea, content, and context. The inspiration with the culture of a city or place is visible in the materials used, which are connected with the history or tradition of a place. Another related approach is inspiration by forms connected with a given culture. Another approach is taken by designers who decide to cut themselves off from the local traditions by introducing into the context a structure that is formally removed from its surroundings. The new structure may be a leaven of novelty – an impulse which will cause changes in the surroundings – and, as a result, change the context.

The concept is also most often a basis for the selection of the materiality of a building, and this choice often goes beyond the purely functional framework. The examples compared in the work in showing the essence of the curtain wall illustrate how important the selection of architectural materiality is for the architectural concept. The concept of the curtain wall does not always depict the "materiality" of contemporary architecture. More often than not, the elevation becomes, in the words of Toyo Ito, a *dress* that covers up the construction materiality of the building.

In creating a building or in the process of designing, it is important to maintain continuity of thought. This continuity gives the solution cohesiveness and distinguishes the structure, creating its individual property. The building becomes recognizable – this is what separates architecture from simple construction.[123] Peter Zumthor expressed this thought in a very simple way in saying, "I believe that every design has a characteristic feature. It must be formulated in a very distinct way so that the whole building can be explained with the help of this basic feature."[124]

The dependence of the decision of the designer on the investor has currently become much greater than in the past. When a commission is accepted from one of these groups, generally a political or a social decision is made. As a result, this determines the direction of architectural thought and their implementation. Despite the complexity of the process of thought development in architecture, a specific cohesiveness is visible, thanks to which architects remain in their area of selected ideas or formal solutions. This continuity of thought in architecture is created thanks to the fact that in every period in history there has always existed a select group of architects-individualists. Dependent on the knowledge, talent, and culture presented in their work but independent of pressure and reliance on the investor. This allows them to preserve autonomy of thought in architectural activities. Many of them can be found among the recipients of the Pritzker Prize.

Therefore, architecture is an integral work which is created to bring joy to human eyes, while the continuity of thought in architecture is best expressed in the constant drive for functional perfection and in maintaining the faith in the beauty of the created buildings.

Notes

1. M. Skaza, *Odkrywając fenomen La Tourette*, www.archsarp.pl/3387/odkrywajac-fenomen-la-tourette [access: 05.05.2021].
2. Personal studies, in situ, March 1982, M. Piotrowski, *La Tourette, czyli co betonowy klasztor mówi o modernizmie*, http://onowymodernizm.pl/la-tourette [access: 06.05.2021].
3. cf. Frank Lloyd Wright, *Modern Architecture. Lectures*, transl. by D. Żukowski, Cracow 2016.
4. "Looks Like a Protestant Barn", https://nyc-architecture.com/UES/UES080.htm [access: 15.04.2021].
5. The building is visible in such films as *Three Days of the Condor* (1975), *Men in Black* (1997), or *The International* (2009).
6. Charles Jencks, "*Modern Movements in Architecture*, transl. by A. Morawińska, H. Palikowska, Warsaw 1987.
7. Ibid., p. 40.
8. Ibid., p. 42.
9. Ibid.
10. Ibid., p. 55.
11. Ibid., p. 61.
12. Ibid., p. 65.
13. Ibid., pp. 67–85.
14. Ibid., p. 91.
15. Ibid., pp. 36–108.
16. Many implementations of this design were completed in Pakistan, Brazil, Egypt, and Western Africa. In Europe and America, this solution was not often used. Cf. P. Gössel, G. Leuthäser, *Architecture in the 20th Century*, transl. by K. Frankowska, L. Głuchowska, Cologne 2006, p. 3.
17. Ibid., p. 350, as well as *Trans World Airlines Flight Center (Now TWA Terminal A) At New York International Airport, Landmarks Preservation Commission*, p. 6, www.neighborhoodpreservationcenter.org/db/bb_files/TWA023.pdf 6 [access: 15.05.2021].
18. Consiglieri L., Consiglieri V, Morphocontinuity in the Work of Eero Saarinen, in: *Recalling Eero Saarinen 1910–2010*, eds. K. Williams, J.M. Rees. "Nexus Network Journal" 2010, vol. 12, no. 2, [e-book] pp. 239–247.
19. C. Siegel, *Structure and Form in Modern Architecture*, transl. by E. Piliszek, Warsaw 1974, p. 232.
20. Ibid.
21. R. Weston, *Plans, Sections, and Elevations. Key Buildings of the Twentieth Century*. London 2004, p. 132.
22. C. Siegel, *Structure and Form . . .*, p. 232 and P. Gössel, G. Leuthäser, *Architecture . . .*, p. 352 and *Trans World Airlines . . .*, p. 6.
23. *Trans World Airlines . . .*, p. 5.

24 *Hotel u Kennedy'ego*, Tvn24bis.pl/wiadomości-gospodarcze, 74/hotel-u-kennedy-ego,161294.html [access: 15.04.2021].
25 I. Meissner, E. Möller, *Frei Otto. Forschen, bauen, inspirieren*, Munich 2015, pp. 9–34 and M. Emmer, Architecture and Mathematics: Soap Bubbles and Soap Films. in: K. Williams, M.J. Ostwald, *Architecture and Mathematics from Antiquity to the Future*, vol. 2, eds. K. Williams, M.J. Ostwald, Cham 2015, pp. 454–455.
26 The Pritzker Architecture Prize: *Biography*, www.pritzkerprize.com/2015/biography [access: 15.05.2021] and N. Yunis, *Frei Otto and the Importance of Experimentation in Architecture*, www.archdaily.com/610531/frei-otto-and-the-importance-of-experimentation-in-architecture [access: 15.05.2021].
27 In 1961, Frei Otto, along with the biologist and anthropologist Johann-Gerhard Helmcke, established the scientific group Biology and Nature. It dealt with, among other things, the study of biomorphic construction of diatoms (a type of algae). These studies were an inspiration for Otto's designs and structures. See: P. Gössel (ed.), *Moderne Architektur A-Z*, vol. 2, Köln 2007, p. 745.
28 J. T. Franco, *Video: Frei Otto's German Pavilion at Expo 67*, www.archdaily.com/607952/video-frei-otto-s-german-pavilion-at-expo-1967/Archdaily, [access: 15.08.2021].
29 The model is visible in the film *F. Otto: The German Pavilion – Expo 1967* made by the Institute for Lightweight Structures of the University of Stuttgart, www.youtube.com/watch?t=113&v=Z0mtFMoseUk [access: 15.05.2021].
30 P. Gössel, G. Leuthäser, *Architecture in the XX century*, vol. 2, Cologne 2010, p. 453.
31 M. Hell, *München '72. Olimpia-Architektur damals und heute*, Munich 2012, pp. 27–30.
32 A. Kroll, *AD Classics: Munich Olympic Stadium/Frei Otto & Gunther Behnisch*, 11.02.2011, www.archdaily.com/?p=109136 [access: 17.05.2021].
33 P. Schumacher, The Congeniality of Architecture and Engineering. The Future Potential and Relevance of Shell Structures in Architecture, London 2013, in: *Shell Structures for Architecture. Form Finding and Optimization*, eds. Sigrid Adriaenssens, Philippe Block, Diederik Veenendaal, Chris Williams, New York 2014.
34 P. Gössel, G. Leuthäser, *Architecture . . .* ibid., pp. 363–379 and J. Rabiej, *Architektura. Sztuka Transfiguracji*, Gliwice 2013, p. 173.
35 E. Węcławowicz-Gyurkovich, *Architektura najnowsza w środowisku miast historycznych*, Cracow 2013, pp. 169–170 and J. Rabiej, *Architektura . . .* ibid., p. 144.
36 Ibid, pp. 93–95.
37 C. Jencks, *The Architecture of the Jumping Universe: A Polemic: How Complexity Science Is Changing Architecture and Culture*, Chichester and London 1995, p. 14.
38 E. Węcławowicz-Gyurkovich, *Architektura najnowsza . . .* ibid., pp. 169–170.
39 B. van Berkel, C. Bos, *UN Studio Designmodelle Architektur Urbanismus Infrastruktur*, Zürich 2006, pp. 150–155.
40 D. Kozłowski, Architektura i przemijanie, in: *Definiowania przestrzeni architektonicznej* "Czasopismo Techniczne" 2011, vol. 4, p. 208.
41 D. Dutton, *The Art Instinct . . .*.
42 M. Bailey, *The Bilbao Effect*, www.forbes.com/2002/02/20/0220conn.html [access: 11.2015].
43 A. Rossi, *The Pritzker Prize Laureates in Their Own Words*, London 2010, p. 236.
44 Ibid.
45 *Aldo Rossi of Italy Elected 1990 Pritzker Architecture Prize Laureate*, www.pritzkerprize.com/laureates/1990# [access: 11.06.2021].
46 P. Gössel, G. Leuthäser, *Architecture . . .*, pp. 439–443.

47 N. Juzwa, A. Gil, *Współczesne postrzeganie architektury: idea – obiekt, narzędzie tworzywo* "Czasopismo Techniczne", Kraków 2006, vol. 9, no. 103, pp. 42–47, N.J. private in situ studies, 2005.
48 P. Jodidio, *Calatrava*, Cologne 2016, pp. 76–79.
49 An interview for *The Wall Street Journal* in 2011: *Frank Gehry A Sit-Down with the Artist of Architecture*, www.wsj.com/articles/SB10001424052748704474804 576222872016570928 [access: 11.06.2021]. The 8 Spruce Street Building functions on the real estate market as "New York by Gehry" https://newyorkbygehry.com/ [access: 11.06.2021].
50 Jan Słyk, *Źródła Architektury informacyjnej*, Warsaw 2012, pp. 159–161.
51 *Ewolucja ściany osłonowej na przykładzie pawilonów EKSPO*, T. Krotowski, Ph. D., dissertation under the tutelage of N. Juzwa, The Lodz University of Technology, 2016.
52 N. Juzwa (ed.), *Architektura współczesnego przemysłu*, Gliwice 2010, p. 129.
53 Ibid.
54 P. Gössel, G. Leuthäser, *Architecture...*, p. 531.
55 K. Kuma et al., *LVMH Osaka*, https://kkaa.co.jp/works/architecture/lvmh-osaka/ [access: 11.06.2021].
56 *Architektura współczesnego przemysłu...*, p. 115.
57 Due to the examples discussed in our work, which are mainly public utility buildings, we have limited ourselves in the tradition of material to stone and ceramics.
58 The Pritzker Architecture Prize, *Jury Citation Wang Shu*, www.pritzkerprize.com/jury-citation-wang-shu [access: 11.12.2019].
59 Ibid.
60 L. Niemojewski, *Uczniowie cieśli (Rozważania nad zawodem architekta)*, Warsaw 1947 (reprint 1999) pp. 6, 7.
61 N. Juzwa, T. Krotowski, Sketch – Computer -Imagination, in: *Computing for a Better Tomorrow*, eds. A. Kępczyńska-Walczak, S. Białkowski, Lodz 2018.
62 See L. Dushkes, *The Architect Says Quotes, Quips and Words of Wisdom*, New York 2012, p. 118.
63 Jan Słyk, *Modele architektoniczne*, Warsaw 2018, p. 7.
64 Research by design – a term popularized in the late nineties of the twentieth century through a discussion within the framework of the European Association for Architectural Education Association Europeenne pour l'Enseignement de l'Architecture – EAAE, AEEA. Jørgen Hauberg, *Research by Design – a Research Strategy*, "Architecture & Education Journal" 2011, no. 5, pp. 46–56.
65 Ibid.
66 D. Kozłowski, *W świecie fikcji, opery, wspaniałego kłamstwa i betonu*, http://architekturabetonowa.pl/aktualności/1257/wświecie-fikcji-opery-wspaniałego-kłamstwa-i-betonu/ [access: 04.05.2021].
67 D.A. Schön, *The Reflective Practitioner. How Professionals Think in Action*, London 1983.
68 M. Sveiven, *AD Classics. Sendai Mediatheque/Toyo Ito & Associates*, www.archdaily.com/118627/ad-classics-sendai-mediatheque-toyo-ito [access: 11.06.2021].
69 See C. Jencks, *Modern Movements...* ibid., p. 66, About Hans Hollein in "Arts and Architecture" 2008, p. 14.
70 M. Mróz, *Popchnąc świat do przodu – Helmut Jahn i jego klasyczny modernizm*, https://internityhome.pl/ih4/popchnac-swiat-przodu-helmut-jahn-klasyczny-modernizm/ [access: 05.01.2020].
71 M. Mróz, *"Uczynić świat lepszym" – an interview with Helmut Jahn*, Sztukaarchitektury.pl/article/4745/8222uczynic.swiat.lepszym.8221-wywiadzhelmutem.jahn.nem/ [access: 04.05.2021].
72 Prof. Dariusz Kozłowski, PhD., Eng., laureate of the SARP Honorary Award in 2011, together with Wacław Stefański and Maria Misiagiewicz, authors of the

architectural complex of buildings of the Higher Theological Seminary of the Resurrectionist Congregation in Cracow.
73 D. Kozłowski in interview with M. Mozga-Górecka, *Zawód architekt: Dariusz Kozłowski*, https://architektura.muratorplus.pl/architektura25/zawod-architekt-dariusz-kozlowski_3886.html [access: 04.05.2021].
74 Ibid.
75 Ibid.
76 Ibid.
77 Jems Architekci: Olgierd Jagiełło, Jerzy Szczepanik-Dzikowski, Maciej Miłobędzki, Wojciech Zych and partners Marcin Sadowski, Paweł Majkusiak, Andrzej Sidorowicz, Marek Moskal.
78 http://jems.pl/onas/ [access: 04.05.2021].
79 Bolesław Stelmach PhD., Eng., the laureate of numerous prizes, including the SARP Honorary Award 2010, awarded the Officer's Cross of the Order of Polonia Restituta (2015), The "Gloria Artis" Bronze Medal for Merit to Culture of the Ministry of Culture and National Heritage.
80 B. Stelmach in interview conducted by D. Bartoszewicz, T. Urzykowski, *Nowa Żelazowa Wola. Piękna i nowoczesna!* www.domiporta.pl/poradnik/1,126867,7880998,Nowa_Zelazowa_Wola__Piekna_i_nowoczesna_.html [access: 15.01.2023].
81 A laureate of national and international prizes for his design and completion of the NOSPR building (Narodowa Orkiestra Symofniczna Polskiego Radia – Polish National Radio Symphony Orchestra) in Katowice, the Prize of the Minister of National Heritage 2014, the Main Prize of the European Commercial Prosperity Awards in the Public Service category, the Silesian Quality Award, The "Gloria Artis" Silver Medal for Merit to Culture, The Medal of the Centenary of the Regaining of Polish Independence awarded by the Prime Minister in 2019.
82 P. Pięciak, *Wierzę w ludzi i marzę*, https//architekturabetonowa.pl/aktualności/1060/wierze-w-ludzi-i-marze [access: 04.05.2021].
83 Prof. Marek Budzyński – the author of numerous important public utility buildings. A laureate of SARP Honorary Award in 1993. In 2014, he was awarded the Commander's Cross of the Order of Polonia Restituta.
84 M. Budzyński in interview with M. Liczbarski, *Budować z myślą o człowieku. An interview with Prof. Marek Budzyński*, www.national-geographic.pl/ludzie/budowac-z-mysla-o-czlowieku-wywiad-z-prof-markiem-budzynskim [access: 04.05.2021].
85 H.-G. Gadamer, *Truth and Method*...
86 Gelernter Mark, *Sources of Architectural Form. A Critical History of Western Design Theory*, Manchester and New York 1995, pp. 5–19.
87 Ibid, p. 7.
88 Ibid.
89 T. Dyckhoff, *The Age of Spectacle: Adventures in Architecture and the 21st-Century City*, transl. by A. Rasmus-Zgorzelska, Cracow 2018, p. 21.
90 Charles Jencks, *Ecstatic Architecture. The Surprising Link*, New York 1999.
91 Ibid.
92 Ibid., pp. 8–23.
93 T. Dyckhoff, *The Age of Spectacle*...
94 Ibid, pp. 7–8.
95 Ibid., p. 14, Underlining by the authors of the book. Translated from the polish edition.
96 The title of T. Dyckhoff's book chapter was used: *The Age of Spectacle*...

97 N. Juzwa, Pragmatism or Emotion? The Sources of Architectural Form, in: *Defining the Architectural Space: Rationalistic or Intuitive Way to Architecture: Monograph*, ed. D. Kozłowski, vol. 1, Cracow 2018, pp. 59–64.
98 Ibid. and private studies by N. Juzwa.
99 See. T. Konior", *Ewolucja domów dla muzyki. Koncept. Kontekst. Architektura*, PhD dissertation, thesis supervisor: N. Juzwa, Lodz University of Technology 2019, also Tomasz Konior in an interview with P. Kozaniecki, B. Paturej, *Tomasz Konior. Dziecko modernizmu w potrzasku*, https://wiadomosci.onet.pl/tylko-w-onecie/tomasz-konior-dziecko-modernizmu-w-potrzasku-wywiad/5devzd [access: 11.06.2021].
100 Plan and cross section are shown in Part 3, "Presentation of Polish Examples."
101 A reference to the title of the film *Pearl in the Crown*, directed by K. Kutz, 1971.
102 NOSPR is part of a network of 21 opinion-making institutions in the European classical music community. In order to be admitted, "*an invitation*" is required. NOSPR was invited by the artistic director of the Elbphilharmonie in Hamburg Christoph Lieben-Seutter.
103 C. Jenks, *The Iconic Building*, New York 2005.
104 The quote is attributed to A. Gaudi.
105 R. de Graff, *Four Walls, and a Roof*, transl. by G. Piątek, Warsaw and Cracow 2019.
106 Such words can be heard in the statements of numerous architects, also those quoted in this book.
107 M. du Sautoy, *The Creativity Code. Art and Innovation in the Age of AI* 2020, transl. by T. Chawziuk, Cracow 2020, p. 10.
108 Ibid., pp. 15–19.
109 Ibid., p. 16.
110 Ibid., p. 17.
111 Ibid., pp. 17–19.
112 Ibid.
113 P. Gössel, G. Leuthäuser, *Architecture . . .*, vol. 2, pp. 531–535.
114 *The Therme Vals/Peter Zumthor*, www.archdaily.com/13358/the-therme-vals [access: 30.08.2019].
115 *Rolex Learning Center*/SANAA, www.archdaily.com/50235/ [access: 19.12.2014].
116 *Le Rolex Center* http://rolexlearningcenter.epfl.ch/ [access: 19.12.2014].
117 Information for the press, published on 01.06.2010 by the Ecole Polytechnique Federale De Lausanne rolexlearningcenter.epfl.ch/files/content/sites/rolexlearningcenter/files/press%20kit/ENGLISH%20Kit2012.pdf [access: 11.06.2021].
118 P. Blundell Jones, *Parc de La Villette in Paris, France by Bernard Tschumi*, www.architectural-review.com/buildings/parc-de-la-villette-in-paris-france-by-bernard-tschumi/8630513.article [access: 14.06.2021].
119 Ibid.
120 Ibid.
121 B. Tschumi, *Event Cities 3: Concept vs. Context vs. Content*, London 2005 [See] teoriaarchitektury.blogspot.com/2013/08/bernard-tschumi-concept-context-content [access: 14.06.2021].
122 Ibid.
123 B. Tschumi, *Event Cities 3* . . ..
124 N. Saieh, *Multiplicity and Memory. Talking About Architecture with Peter Zumthor*, www.archdaily.com/85656/multiplicity-and-memory-talking-about-architecture-with-peter-zumthor [access: 18.05.2021].

Part II Value, Beauty, and Place

Part II of our thoughts on architecture in innovative contemporaneity is dedicated to user-friendly architecture. It shows the problem of city space, in which the *place*, thanks to the development and the completion of high-quality structures, becomes a space that is important for the inhabitants.

On User-Friendly Architecture: Three Examples

In creating the material environment of our surroundings, architecture enters most strongly into the needs of everyday life. However, in the architectural recording of value, buildings with a greater significance are those that serve to emphasize the prestige of authority or elevate the meaning of culture, religion, or science. In following this trend, we begin Part II with a presentation of three examples. The Oslo Opera House, designed by Snøhetta, 2007, and the building of the New Museum of Contemporary Art in New York, designed by SANAA, 2005, relate a beautiful story of values that are embedded in the architecture, but also of how architecture can change a place, making it friendly for people. The third example shows a transformation of a post-industrial area damaged by human activity into a user-friendly location.

The Oslo Opera House, 2007, by Snøhetta, is situated in the eastern part of the city center, on the waterfront. The construction of the Opera was the first stage of the transformation of the Bjørvika district. Apart from the planned location where opera plays and classical music spectacles would take place, the building was to play an important role in the restoration of the district. Functionally connecting the area of the location of the new building with the waterfront required moving car traffic into the tunnel. The surface, recovered in this way, was transformed into city squares and a promenade for pedestrians.[1]

Both the competition design as well as the completed building possess three basic elements of architectural composition, referred to by the architects as the wave wall, the factory, and the carpet.

DOI: 10.4324/9781003413561-3

"The wave wall" is a border between the generally accessible part of the Opera and the parts that require the purchase of a ticket. In the mind of the architects, the wall symbolizes the meeting point of sea and land, as well as of people and culture. It is a reference to the port history of the city, where the port was a boundary between Oslo and the rest of the world: "The Bjørvika Peninsula is part of a harbor city, historically the meeting point with the rest of the world. The dividing line between the ground 'here' and the water 'there' is both a real and a symbolic threshold."[2]

"The factory" is the manufacturing part of the Opera, a part that is quite developed, with approximately 600 people, representing 50 different professions, working inside.[3]

"The carpet" is a sculpturally shaped continuous surface that connects the roof with the sea but is also a generally accessible public space. In addition to the architects from Snøhetta, the form of the roof was a response to the question posed in the competition on creating a monumental structure. The feature that the authors wanted to emphasize in this monumental building was the idea of community and meetings between residents. Space that is accessible to everyone, not through the aid of a vertical element, but through a traditionally shaped form, is "the carpet" – meaning, the surface of the roof. Independent of the events taking place inside the building, the roof, "the carpet" has become an attractive, frequently visited hangout for Oslo inhabitants, while the majestic building has become a symbol of the restored district. The aforementioned description does not fully show the significance and exceptionality of the architecture completed by Snøhetta. According to the designer Kjetil T. Thorsen, the Oslo Opera House is both a landscape and an architecture. The form is an urban link and not "a divisive expressive sculpture."[4] The exceptional way in which music can be enjoyed in the Opera points to the serving role of architecture in a structure designated for music. The most important source of the form of this building is its functionality.

The generally accessible spaces inside the building as well as the accessibility of external spaces cause the structure to fulfill the expected social tasks. It is an attractive location to spend time, not only for music enthusiasts. Thanks to the generally accessible surfaces of the roof, which seems to surround the hall from all sides, the hall itself takes on a three-dimensional landscape character. In quoting Denise Scott Brown, we would have said, "[A]rchitecture cannot force people to connect, it can only plan the crossing points, remove the barriers, and make meeting places useful and attractive."[5]

The New Museum of Contemporary Art building in New York, 2007, designed by SANAA, was created in a dilapidated nineteenth-century district on Lower Manhattan. The form of the building is reminiscent of boxes carelessly placed one on top of the other, up to 53 m high. The esthetics of the structure is harmonious and unexpectedly simple, despite the functional complexity of the museum building. The task of the structure was to create space that would integrate the community of the district and aid in the spatial restoration of the street and, in the end, the entire district. The museum function was extended to include an educational center, shops, a theater hall, a space for large events and happenings, as well as a terrace on the roof. It occupies seven stories, which are made up of "boxes" of various heights. The first four house the entrance lobby, a bookshop, restaurants, and museum galleries. As the authors say, these boxes are supposed to symbolize clashing and constantly moving creative ideas of contemporary art.[6] The museum building is separated from traffic by a glass wall over 4 m high that allows passers-by to look inside. The reinforced concrete and steel construction of the building allowed for obtaining a pillarless surface of the museum interiors. The idea of the architects was to create a building that would reflect the twenty-first century with all its potential. One of the most important elements of the concept was mesh lathing used on the façade walls. Its task was not to show what was happening inside; rather, it was an inspiration for the designers. It became a demonstration of something new – the innovativeness of the structure.

The architects from SANAA emphasize the fact that using a mesh lathing, a material commonly used in industry, had a more of a poetic significance. It was of a symbolic character, which served to underline the value of the durability of the material. In the end, it was decided to use aluminum mesh instead of steel mesh. This allowed for the creation of a very contemporary form, which in addition obtained a more subtle, delicate character.[7] The architects from SANAA, recipients of the Pritzker Prize in 2010, in expressing their opinion, say, "We have always been attracted by this ambivalence between something and nothing, by this floating identity of materials and space."[8] Right next to the building designed by SANAA, an extension of the museum is planned, designed by the OMA design studio. Thanks to this decision, the museum will have an additional 5,000 m^2 of new surface area.[9] The new museum fulfills its basic goal – the task of renewal of the social community of the district.

The European Rekula Project of the restoration of a post-industrial area in Lower Lusatia seems to be a topic from a different domain. It concerns the revitalization of a post-industrial area situated near the southern borders of Berlin. The IBA Program (Internationale Bauaustellung Fuerst Pueckerland),[10] 2000–2010, was supposed to restore the utility value of land that was damaged and degraded by the mining industry and the investments that accompanied it.

The initiator, as well as the leader of the IBA project, was the town planner Rolf Kuhn.[11] The idea of the program was for the area to be transformed into a land of lakes, a place for relaxation for the inhabitants of nearby Berlin. These dreams were fulfilled due to the inclusion of spectacular actions from the border of art into the IBA program, which took advantage of the already-useless industrial machines. Here we present two of these actions which were closest to architecture, as well as close to the connections between art and architecture.[12] Both take advantage of the change of the use of technical devices into structures of art.

- The silos of the shut down Lauchhammer coking plant, known as Biotowers, are over 20 m high towers, which in the past served industrial technology. Today the structure is closed down, while the towers, spaced around in an irregular row, are reminiscent of a huge sculpture in form. Thanks to the introduction of lighting into the building, the form changes shape, creating a new, strange, captivating place, one that is willingly visited by the inhabitants of the city. When, in their opinion, the towers became a work of art, the building was renamed Castel del Monte of Lusatia, and visitors had to pay to get in.
- The F60 Project, which was tasked with creating a new image of "the place," used the form of an enormous idle excavator. After the mine was shut down, steel construction of over 500 m in length remained, being referred to by residents as "lying Eiffel Tower." It was transformed into a large sculpture, which, elevated above the artificially created lake, serves as a playground for children. The only thing needed to transform this huge useless construction into a work of art was "an artist's touch."[13]

Figure 2.1 The Silesian Museum, Riegler Riewe Architekten, Katowice, 2012.
Source: Dominika Warczyńska.

52 *Value, Beauty, and Place*

The authors of the IBA project, in bestowing the value of art to technical devices that have lost their usability, brought back memories of painting, which has, for many centuries, amazed us with the beauty of the images of items of everyday use.

Changing old industrial buildings into objects of art, the authors of the project brought to the forefront an ongoing discussion about the value of a *ready-made* object in art. Let us briefly summarize the presented examples. The contemporary image of the Castel del Monte of Lusatia, with its nonstandard beauty of form, relates to the famous term used by Corbusier, "the play of volumes brought together in light," which points to the attributes or the principal feature of contemporary architecture. The huge construction of the F60 excavator, which reminded the inhabitants of a "lying Eiffel Tower," is a permission to show a Polish example. The designers of the Silesian Museum in Katowice, using the charm of the former trestle shaft, changed its usage, transforming it into a viewing deck. Now, the shaft tower serves the inhabitants to soar upwards to admire the beauty of "the place." Moreover, the old structure blends in perfectly with the glass architecture of the museum's more recent years.

On Value and Beauty in Architecture

Value

Value in architecture takes on a diverse character; it may be utility, historical, scientific, spatial, artistic, or others. In layman's terms, *value* is associated with a cost which we must incur to acquire a given item. However, when the topic in question is architectural space, such a strictly economic understanding of value becomes impossible. Space in architecture created for human utility needs possesses a very diverse character. It is strongly connected with the emotionality of human sensations; thus, it cannot be brought down to measurable dimensions. That is why it is important to introduce a division into measurable and non-measurable values.

In the book *Archiektura i wartość* (*Architecture and Value*) by Andrzej Basista,[14] the author presents a clear division of values present in architecture. We see a table divided into two columns: the first one lists utility values – technical, functional, and ethical – while the second, cultural and artistic values. Apart from those that fit the category of utility values, most of them are non-measurable values. The author includes "beauty" in the non-measurable category, connected with culture.

In the process of shaping or evaluating a work of art, value, even taking into account fields seemingly not linked with architecture, still has a great significance. This occurs when an architectural image of a building becomes an element of contemporary commercial marketing. Then, to present the values of the product being sold, we often use the architectural image of the building of the company that produces a given good. This is clearly visible in constructing the identity of large corporations, for example, Apple, and is even present in the architecture of industrial buildings in which the quality of formal solutions becomes a sort of confirmation of the quality of the manufactured product.[15] A good example of this is the Vacheron Constantin factory, by Bernard Tschumi, 2004, in which elegant watches of the Cartier brand are produced. The architecture of the structure, but most of all "the arrogantly" bent line of the roof, seems to confirm the fact that the building is a guarantee not only of beauty but also of the manufactured product. The image of the building attracts the client, influences the way the factory is perceived, despite the fact that according to public opinion, it is not architecturally attractive. This more and more visible inclusion of architecture into the marketing function is becoming one of the features of innovative contemporaneity.

The current way of shaping and implementing structures with an extended function, such as city centers, shopping centers, and academic and scientific facilities, causes buildings to be created as a result of a more and more complicated process of design and increased participation from various expert groups.

A large group of people influences the shape, beauty, and utility of the developed structure, including architects and urban planners, developers, constructors, installers, and representatives of other industries. At the same time, architecture can only come into existence when a need for it arises, when a business plan is developed. In quoting Tom Dyckhoff: "In the end buildings are business."[16]

The economic dimension of architecture and the presence of many people from different industries mean that although architecture is part of culture, in the category of art, it finds itself in a rather lowly pace, behind other fields, such as painting, sculpture, photography.

For the average building user, it is comfort and quality of utility that are the most important. Only after these needs are satisfied – the creation of a new, material quality means – that the building or urban arrangements possess a cultural dimension. In the interview quoted earlier, the outstanding architect Helmut Jahn says that the utility of a building is sometimes even more important that architectural esthetics;[17] among architects, such a view is rather common. The evaluation of non-measurable values is difficult, since it concerns categories of beauty and esthetics, and thus, in such situations, it focuses on comparative research. Generally, this value serves various purposes, including becoming the basis of making decisions to keep, transform, or destroy existing structures. Architecture that is destroyed is one that has lost its value. A new building is expected to better fulfill the expectations of the users. Along with Zbigniew Paszkowski,[18] we may think about the length of the duration of value and pose the question: Is it possible for timeless values to exist in a more and more rapidly changing image of reality?

If we are to compare the duration period of classicist ideas that lasted until contemporary times, a clear acceleration of the occurring changes is visible. Agreeing with the author that in architecture, timeless value most often occurs thanks to hidden symbolism, thanks to the identity of a place, or thanks to collective memory, let us add that timeless value is also visible in works that are distinguished by individual artistry and the architect's creativity. The currently developed media system of data transfer transfers information regarding new achievements in architectural creation faster than ever before. Yet still, timeless architectural works are simpler to notice and define in a historical context. Such buildings depict important stages of the development of civilization, generally becoming an image and a symbol of a place, but also of the time when they were created.

When speaking about values in architecture, similarly to fashion, we can speak of everyday fashion, known as *quotidienne*, or about fashion referred to as *haute couture*, which set the trends or tendencies in the style of our fashion. In keeping with French, another word that should be added is *parfois*, meaning "sometimes" or "not often." *Parfois* also reflects the need for beauty in dress. We can speak about architecture in the same way when it fulfills our everyday needs: life, work, education, health, and others. The architecture of such buildings possesses a definite utility, which is the basis of the value of the building. We also construct buildings that are visited by us occasionally – infrequently, or from time to time, meaning *parfois*. However, in these buildings, we would also like to experience the beauty of the architectural harmony of place.

Besides the ones already mentioned, there are also buildings created that, possessing the feature of formal uncommonness, create a surprisingly new quality of space. Generally, these are buildings that fulfill "higher-order values" in our lives.

In the subject literature, in order to evaluate such specific buildings, the term *Gesamtkunstwerk* was created, meaning, a work that is perfect in its entirety and in all its details. Buildings that are distinguished in such a way are those that amaze us and/or those that receive awards, beginning with the European Mies van der Rohe Award, which was received by the Mieczysław Karłowicz Philharmonic in Szczecin, 2014, designed by the Spanish architects Fabrizio Barozzi and Alberto Veiga.

The most important award for establishing value in architecture is the Pritzker Prize, also known as the architectural Nobel. It has been awarded annually for the last 40 years, reflecting utility perfection and esthetics of formal solutions. In 2019, this highest distinction in architecture was given to a Japanese architect, Arata Isozaki, who is also the author of the Manggha Museum of Japanese Art and Technology in Cracow, thus contributing to the elevation of the value of modern Polish architecture.

Value, Beauty, and Place 55

Figure 2.2 Szczecin Philharmonic Symphony Orchestra was awarded the European Mies van der Rohe Award in 2014; Fabrizio Barozzi, Alberto Veiga, Szczecin, 2014.

Source: Kamila Kozioł/Szczecin Philharmonic.

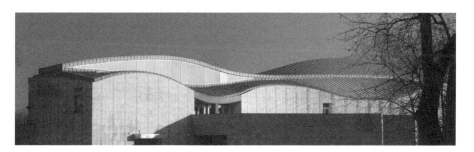

Figure 2.3 Manggha Museum of Japanese Art and Technology in Cracow, Arata Isozaki, 1994. Arata Isozaki received the Pritzker Prize in 2019.

Source: Photo by Krzysztof Ingarden.

Beauty

When thinking about value in architecture, we cannot omit the topic of beauty. Architects most often say that for them the utility of a building is more important than beauty. It seems that they are wrong. Every day, thousands of tourists travel the world in search of architectural beauty. They go to see or touch that one amazing building, to listen to a concert in a famous concert hall, or to sit down for a brief moment near an enchanted square. If we believe that architecture is an activity that is part of culture, within the realm of art, in the initial thought about beauty, we would like to recall a series of articles titled *In Search of Beauty*. It begins with the words of Albrecht Dürer: "A painter whose duty is to paint a picture should paint it as beautifully as he is able to. However, what beauty is, I know not."[19] If we were to paraphrase his statement and apply it to beauty in architecture, we could say that the beauty of a structure depends on the talent of an architect; therefore, we must entrust its design to a master.

Professor Semir Zeki, the creator of a new field of neuroesthetics, says that beauty is a key part of our life; "it is so important that we spend a great deal of money on it." Listing various kinds of beauty, he points out that there is "the beauty of art, but there is also beauty in mathematics, which we look for in order to understand the structure of the universe."[20] Beauty can vary, or it can be defined in multiple ways. When we enter the term *beauty* into Google, we get a significant number of websites, of which most deal with the beauty of hairstyles or dress as well as a growing number of accessories. This excess is an expression of a life supervised and controlled by the contemporary consumer market, in which beauty "becomes a recipe for anxiety and constant hurry."[21] Nevertheless, beauty in architecture, next to utility, seems to be a value of key importance.

If we ponder beauty in architecture, two thoughts come to mind: understanding beauty and . . . searching for beauty in architecture.[22]

Understanding Beauty

Our feelings on the beauty of a place are non-measurable. Beauty is an important quality, not only for the development of culture, but also in the aspect of economic development.

The aforementioned Semir Zeki quotes a letter from a young Japanese who writes about his feelings when he first witnessed Michelangelo's sculpture *The Pietà*. A face-to-face meeting with beauty caused him to be moved to tears. This was a young man's first encounter with an unknown, foreign to him, Christian culture.[23] This story shows a great, timeless, but also supracultural significance of beauty. This is also perfectly expressed by the thought of Gadamer, quoted in the introduction of the book: "Everything that is not part of the necessities of life but is concerned with the 'how' . . ."

We may speak of two kinds of beauty: of biological beauty, such as beautiful faces, beautiful landscapes, as well as of artificial beauty, such as the beauty of a car, beauty of a building. Biological beauty is very resistant to cultural influences; however, artificial beauty is subject to them to a higher degree. Therefore, it should come as no surprise that Europeans generally prefer the beauty of buildings created in the Western culture.[24] If art, painting, sculpture, and architecture are to be included in the same, or similar, category, we may repeat the words of Anda Rottenberg. She believes that in contemporary art, "the category of beauty has been replaced by a category of understanding and that we generally get these two things confused. People generally believe that beauty is that which can be understood."[25] It should be added that generally, that which is understood is part of our own culture.

Beauty is a migrating category. Something which has not been universalized is not believed to be beautiful. Works, which are outside the approved canon, are not thought of as beautiful until they have been universalized, and then they become part of a new canon, after which they stop being fashionable and once again become ugly. Later, they come back once again, except that they have been somewhat "cleansed" by history.[26]

That is according to Anda Rottenberg, art critic, author of many books and essays on art. There seems to be much truth in these words, which can be applied to the perception of beauty in architecture. The value of an object, and therefore also the value of beauty, is commonly equivalent to its price. However, in an axiological discussion, we do not talk about price. On the other hand, thoughts on beauty as a value, which is the particular quality of an object experienced by people, are interesting, indeed. This value seems to be invariable; only the possibilities of its cognition vary.

Beauty? In ancient Greece, the concept of beauty was connected with morality, thought, and mind. In the words of Władysław Tatarkiewicz:

> [B]eauty is a positive esthetic attribute of being, which results from maintaining proportions, a harmony of colors, sounds, moderation of utility, experienced by the senses. There is an ideal beauty, a spiritual one, as well as others such as the moral, corporeal, objective, and subjective. A term that is connected with the theory of esthetics, truth, and good. In metaphysics beauty is one of the transcendental properties of being, which expresses its fusion, transparency, internal proportion, as well as perfection.[27]

The problem of beauty used to be the domain of the Church and theologians. Some believed that beauty, in contributing to piousness, is created for the glory of the Creator; others that it is an expression of man's ties to the material worldly goods. Today the old dispute between the beauty of the shining gold and the magnificence of the tabernacle versus the beauty of the simplicity of towers is nothing but a memory, yet the essence is still valid. In the times of contemporarily universal relativism, we believe that "beauty" is a value that is more readily created in the mind of the onlooker than exists in the value of an object in itself.

58 Value, Beauty, and Place

In discussions about architecture, there often appears the topic of beauty as an element that allows for the characterization and/or valuation in the description of a building. Beauty as a criterion of value in architecture has been firmly embedded in philosophical deliberations. Hans-Georg Gadamer believes that beauty is a value that is, above all, other values: time, technical perfection, or utility. This statement means that "beauty" is the ideal criterion of perfection of work.

Max Scheler invokes three traditions from the history of the development of culture: theological, philosophical, and scientific, to which genetic psychology is added. These three traditions are rather incohesive, yet they allow for the presentation of a rather-complete vision of contemporary times, showing unity but, at the same time, dualism of the contemporary "being of man."[28] Scheler created a hierarchy of values in which beauty as an esthetic value is near the top, second among spiritual values, immediately behind absolute values. Beauty also ranks very high in the texts of Roman Ingarden. The Polish phenomenologist ranked beauty second among values of culture, behind moral values, which he placed on the top. Ingarden considers a work of art as an intentional object that exists in layers. For a literary work, he distinguishes four layers: a layer of sounds of words, a layer of meanings, a layer of the appearance of objects, and the layer of the objects, meaning, the content of an artwork. It must be added that Ingarden considers the reader as a co-author of the work.[29] For him, the idealist approach to art is important. The approach of the phenomenologist can be transferred to a work of architecture. However, in searching for beauty in architecture, the ethical dimension of the work, in reference to the search for beauty, seems substantially more complicated than the esthetic dimension.[30]

Thanks to the noticeable utility of a building, but also thanks to formal solutions, the architecture transports the culture of place and time in which it is created. For contemporary buildings, materiality and the technological solutions connected with it are as important as esthetics. The use of matter in a way that is typical for the completion time dates the work and generally also indicates the place of its creation. Similar ideas may be found in the works of Władysław Tatarkiewicz, who, in the beauty of architecture, distinguishes proportions and appropriateness. If by *proportions* he understands architectural form, proportions, and harmony of the interior, also understood as the harmony of the plan as well as integrality of the solutions of the interior and exterior of the spatial arrangements, then *appropriateness* means the functionality of structure, but also ethical and moral values[31] of the building. The already-quoted Anda Rottenberg believes that "contemporary beauty requires understanding, but also familiarization and universalization." This statement is concurrent with the thoughts of Immanuel Kant, who wrote that beauty is "free" from "dependent" beauty,[32] believed that that which is beautiful appeals to everyone and is selfless, separating "judgment of taste" from the concept of perfection. These thoughts, interpreted by Dutton, allow for a statement that is important for architecture, namely, that beauty of a work "is a materialized show of abilities, which requires from us the capture of skills which are put into its creation."[33]

Searching for Beauty in Architecture

We begin the search for the beauty of an architectural work with the thoughts on beauty as a migrating category. Three examples of this are the royal chapel Sainte Chappelle in Paris, thirteenth century; the Bruder Klaus Kapelle, Peter Zumthor, 2006; as well as the small Apple Store in New York, Bohlin Cyvinski, Jackson, 2006, which show the beauty of architecture migrating in the category of time and the category of the functionality of the structure.

Still today, the beauty of the vault painted in blue with the gold lilies of the Bourbons in the royal Saint Chapelle in Paris enhances us. We continue to be captivated by the art of constructing form in the royal Louvre, yet the old courtly canon of beauty is willingly placed opposite the modest field Bruder Klaus Kapelle by Peter Zumthor. And we even dare to compare royal beauty to contemporary beauty, which is expressed by the New York–based Apple Store. The first two examples show beauty that accompanies spirituality, religious feelings. The third one represents the beauty of the contemporary, consumer world.

The Sainte-Chapelle is a personification of traditional, courtly beauty. The interior of the royal chapel, compared with the example of the rural chapel of Peter Zumthor, maintains the still current, traditional canon of beauty but, at the same time, even more strongly emphasizes the otherness of contemporary beauty. This otherness is visible in the simplicity of form, the bold use of wood, this eternal, traditional material, here used in a very unusual form. In order to call this structure art, let us add the talents of its creator, whose contemporary ease of mixing form and content from different sources was emphasized by the speech delivered upon his receipt of the Pritzker Prize: "a cross between Mies van der Rohe and Marcel Proust with perhaps a tiny bit of Bob Dylan thrown in."[34] The third example is a smallish glass hexagon, the Apple Store, which is located in New York, at the busy intersection of Columbus Circle and Fifth Avenue. The architecture of the store shows how the significance and character of beauty change, but at the same time, it shows how the thought on beauty has been democratized. The small glass cube, basically completely devoid of any function, stands "at the foot" of the huge Mercedes building at one of the busier crossroads of NYC. The interior of the glass box amazes us with a complete lack of function; it is a casing of an empty space that houses a glass elevator and a winding glass staircase. Both these glass elements serve as the entrance to the sales floor. The shop itself is located below the glass cubicle. The glass cage of the Apple Store, in which the god of consumerism has found shelter, serves our daily needs but is also an expression of the finesse of contemporary technology. The building seems as if it were bereft of matter, serving as a well-thought-out strategy of creating a vestibule for the entrance to the shop itself. It is reminiscent of the mystery of entering an Orthodox church somewhere on the border between Eastern and Western Europe. There we can also see gates concealing the sanctity of a place. In the Apple Store, subsequent "gates" separate the presentations of tiny computer "wonders" from the prying eyes of a simple passer-by. The previously presented examples show how, in an innovative contemporaneity, the possibilities of searching for beauty in architecture not only democratize but also widen.

Thanks to the visible utility of a building and formal solutions, architecture transports the culture of place and time in which it was created. New, contemporary materiality is shown in architecture, as well as technological solutions connected with it. Matter used in a way that is characteristic for a specific period of completion "dates" the work and generally also shows where it was created. The importance of the integrality of a building with its surroundings is clearly shown by Roman Ingarden,[35] attributing great significance to the ability of the newly designed building to blend into the pre-existing context of its surroundings.

Technical and technological perfection of architecture results in the fact that its connections with business and politics are becoming ever stronger. In the end, architecture is a business in which someone always pays the bills.

Banks, but also other buildings which are linked with the economy, are not only the depositary of costs but also invest in architectural beauty. The marketing function of architecture is becoming an auxiliary factor. Both of the buildings shown in what follows are connected with the transformation of the Polish economy, namely:

- The BRE Bank in Bydgoszcz, 1996, arch. Andrzej Bulanda, Włodzimierz Mucha, a building of uncommon beauty, placed among old granaries and riverfront storehouses, splendidly enriches the city landscape.
- The Warsaw Stock Exchange, 1998–2000, arch. Stanisław Fiszer, Andrzej M. Chołdzyński, a building embedded in the urban tissue of Warsaw, is at the same time a beautiful continuation of the surrounding buildings as well as architectural contemporaneity.

Both the Bydgoszcz-based BRE Bank and the Warsaw Stock Exchange are large-scale buildings. In such buildings, more than in others, it is visible how all components are important for beauty in architecture: proportions, the harmony of the interior, as well as the cohesiveness of architectural solutions of the structure in relation to the pre-existing surroundings.

The harmony and beauty of architecture are of particular importance to buildings, which are part of the public space. These buildings are important for inhabitants due to the social values that they bring to the public space of the city, creating high-quality urbanity. They are important for individuals because they create beauty that accompanies meetings and family outings, elevating the culture of a place. They are important for urban space because they raise the significance of a city in global competition.

The way in which the form of the new building responds to the functional conditions and how it becomes part of the urban space is a result of the concept of the designer-architect. Bernard Tschumi says that the new form may enter into different relations with its surroundings. It can:

- Cooperate with the context of the place
- Be created as a new, independent form
- Sometimes be created as a new form, neutral to the pre-existing context of its surroundings[36]

Figure 2.4 The Krzysztof Kieślowski Film School of the University of Silesia.
Source: Dominika Werczyńska.

The building of the International Congress Center in Katowice, 2015, by JEMS Architekci, to a large extent, owes its architectural beauty to the idea which originated in the history and the mining tradition of Upper Silesia. The great black body of the structure known as the MCK (ICC) is situated near the Spodek (tn. "The Saucer" – a popular sports and entertainment arena) and is reminiscent of a grass-covered slag heap. It is an image of the memory of the Silesian land and its history. The building has not only become a pretext for the creation of new, high-quality congress interiors but has also created a new landscape of a place.[37]

The aforementioned classification by Bernard Tschumi has given the pretext to bring to the forefront yet another group of buildings that are situated in the urban tissue of the city. The buildings, apart from their functionality, are tasked with the elevation of the value of this location. They are, in order of completion: 2008, the Symfonia Center of Musical Science and Education in Katowice, arch. Tomasz Konior and Krzysztof Barysz, Konior Studio; the Małopolska Garden of Art in Cracow, arch. Ingarden and Ewy; 2018, the Krzysztof Kieślowski Film School of the University of Silesia, designed by Grupa 5 Architekci, BAAS, and the detailed design was completed by the Małeccy Design Studio from Katowice.

Three buildings remind us of the idea which is at the top of their conception, one which seems to emerge out of the World Museum of Imagination[38] and which tells the story of the beauty of a façade, which maintains the standard of the regulation line and the ceramic tradition of the region. The buildings tell a tale of the history of a place, and using the words of Dennis Dutton, they are "a materialized show of abilities" of the architectural profession.

The simplicity and elegance of form, as well as the character of the location of the Faculty of the University of Silesia, the Krzysztof Kieślowski Film School in Katowice, bring to mind the New Museum of Contemporary Art in New York and also force us to mention the creators, amazed at the sharpness of contrast of the surroundings in relation to the new architecture. In recalling both locations, we may compare "the mission" which both facilities must carry out.

Place

Space and Place

In history, a city was connected with the concept of the feeling of freedom; for centuries, it has allowed its inhabitants to dream of freedom and independence. Today, when we think of a city, we often speak of space, which satisfies our needs for culture, entertainment, education, and others. These needs, which are seen as higher-order needs, are often created in areas that are distinguished on the urban development plan of a city. Some of them create a place. The quality of this space is expressed by spatial composition, diversity, and beauty of architectural forms – the culture of spatial development; these are features that influence our feeling of satisfaction or disapproval. As controversial as it seems, the oft-quoted by us Peter Zumthor has this to say about quality:

> Quality in architecture – I think, this is not such an intellectual, academic discussion. Atmosphere. Everybody feels it. . . . It is about creating a good building, place, and usage. . . . If an ordinary person thinks it is good, then it means that it is good. People are not stupid.[39]

More and more often we speak of a community that creates the value of city space. In a discussion about the quality of urban solutions, we frequently speak of economic and social factors, which contribute to the shaping of urbanized space, influencing its creation, but also the quality of user-friendly places.

Jan Gehl suggests decreasing car traffic in the central zone of the city. In his books *Cities for People* and *Life Between Buildings*, he reminds us of spaces that are created "between buildings," either not developed or sparsely developed; they become the reason for the disappearance of public life in the city. In undertaking the topic of place, in a way, we join this discussion, beginning it with the definition of space.

Space is an abstract term that contains a rather-complex set of concepts. *Space* in geography means the layer covering the landscape of the ground with its physical diversity; in physics, it means that which surrounds us.[40] Space is open; it suggests the future, but to a lesser and lesser degree, it protects us from danger. Place means stability and safety. Based on the research of an American Chinese professor, Yi Fu Tuan, we may say that "closed and humanized space becomes a place." That is what Yi Fu Tuan has to say about place in his classic description:

> In comparison with space, the place is a calm center of agreed-upon values. . . . In order to appreciate the value of urban landscape its inhabitants . . . need both space, as well as place. . . . In open space, we may experience the values of place more intensively, while in the loneliness of a quiet place the enormity of space becomes a dominant factor.[41]

However, this problem is presented in a similar way by Bohdan Jałowiecki:

> That which is space at the beginning becomes a place as we become familiar with it and bestow it with value. The concepts of space and place need each other. The safety and stability of place directs our attention to the openness, grandeur, and terror of space – and vice versa.[42]

64 *Value, Beauty, and Place*

Public space in a city historically had three main functions. It was a place of:

- Meetings between inhabitants
- Organization of numerous forms of trade
- Connection between various areas of city activities

Jan Gehl believes that the creation of public spaces is an act of "returning the cities to people." In dealing with the problem of "a city for people," he brings to the forefront the topic of the significance of a return to "good, old, urbanity," about which we have forgotten for a moment. He is in favor of restoring and/or creating new public spaces.[43]

Remaining for a moment within the scope of spatial development, it is good to remember that the shaping of place in a city is a process in which it is difficult to unambiguously evaluate the negative or positive effects of real achievements. Most often, this evaluation is relative – we state that a solution is better or worse in comparison with other, similar ones, and also in comparison with the possibilities and the passing time.

In the opinion of architects and city planners, places that are user-friendly concern space with values, which are of a unique and diverse character. A meeting with some of those places will allow us to expand the problem in the context of an architectural structure. These examples show a diversity with which the context of the presented structure is perceived. The way of understanding context generally influences the evaluation of a building both by professionals as well as by ordinary inhabitants of the city. It is therefore relevant that the concept contains clear and valuable references to a broadly understood place, its history, and culture. This allows for the creation of an interesting and surprising architecture, which is further underlined by the words Ewa P. Porębska: "the reinterpretation of heritage is in Poland a leading method of creating unique and valuable architecture."[44] Her words are echoed by Tom Dyckhoff, who reminds us that one of the tasks of architecture is to create places that are accessible, friendly, and which arouse emotions, places that possess their own identity. Such aspects, once subjective, in contemporary times – when architecture becomes the calling card of a place, an institution, and also a city[45] – acquire an economic dimension. Jan Gehl presents the "vitality" or activity of such a space in an interesting way. He notices that it is not the number of people and events but, rather, time – counted in minutes spent outside – that influences the activity of a place. He further observes that, if there are opportunities for an activity that increases the need to be in a certain place from 10 to 20 min, the level of activity of place doubles.[46] For "a place" to be established, the uniqueness of functional combinations is important. Gehl points out that if "space is beautiful, and the details are carefully designed, it is a value in itself."[47] These thoughts have also become important for the selection of the presented examples.

Our presentation of examples begins with Lublin. The great building named the Center for the Meeting of Cultures in Lublin was an image of *a place in the city space*, an image that has become the start or, more appropriately, a true *leaven of thought* on the content of the book's second part.

THE CENTER FOR THE MEETING OF CULTURES IN LUBLIN, 2015

ARCHITECTURE:	Bolesław Stelmach – Stelmach & Partners Architectural Office
Surface Area:	29,800 m²
Investment Cost:	220 M PLN
Design:	2009
Completion:	2015

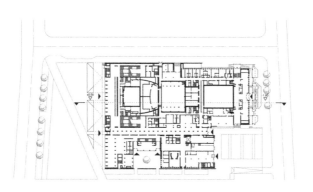

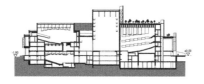

Figure 2.5 The Center for the Meeting of Cultures in Lublin, floor plan and section.
Source: Filip Zamiatnin/book authors.

The completion of the structure known as the Theatre Under Construction lasted 40 years. For financial reasons, the construction was often halted; over the years, the partially completed buildings housed a philharmonic and a musical theater. The unfinished construction of this grand building had, for decades, had a negative influence on the city center.

It was not until 2009, when a competition for the development of an architectural and urban concept of the Center for the Meeting of Cultures[48] was won by

Bolesław Stelmach, that things finally started moving. The enormous structure includes a modern opera hall for 942 persons, a chamber hall for 200 persons, a cinema hall, and a ballet hall.[49] The design used the pre-existing constructions of the structures, which were created during subsequent stages of work on the unfinished facility. The new solutions are, in a visible way, included in the elements of the old structure. Old demolished brick and walls were used. New structures are made out of reinforced concrete of various textures of finishing, partially obtained due to processing by hand. In the architecture of the building, glass plays a significant role. Following the words of Bolesław Stelmach:

> The concept of the building speaks of three layers of the various times of creation and function: Gutenberg's kurgans on the square in front of the building relate to the past, the multimedia elevations symbolize the present, while the hanging gardens on the roofs herald the future of architecture.[50]

Glass in the materiality of the structure fulfills a key role allowing for the penetration of the atmosphere, which is created inside the building, onto the square, around the theater. Thus, there is an extension of the public space that exists around the hall of the interior and its connection with the public space of the city. The green roof of the building plays a similar role, and on the elevation, it is accentuated by glass passages with a panoramic view of the area.

The monumental body of the Center for the Meeting of Cultures brings order to the urban arrangements of the city. By introducing a new, well-organized large public space into the urban structure, it creates a place which, accessible from the level of the square in front of the building, through the interior, is transported to the level of the roof of the building.[51]

Figure 2.6 The Center for the Meeting of Cultures in Lublin, Bolesław Stelmach, Stelmach & Partners Architectural Office, Lublin, 2015.

Source: Marcin Czechowicz/Stelmach & Partners Architectural Office.

THE EUROPEAN SOLIDARITY CENTER IN GDANSK, 2014

ARCHITECTURE:	PPW Fort Architektura Wojciech Targowski
Surface Area:	28,988 m²
Investment Cost:	230 M PLN
Design:	2007–2009
Completion:	2014

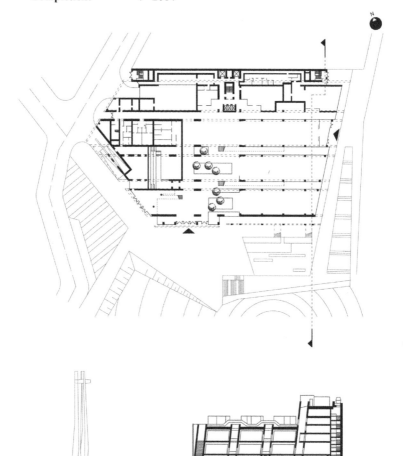

Figure 2.7 The European Solidarity Center in Gdansk, floor plan and section.
Source: Filip Zamiatnin/book authors.

Value, Beauty, and Place 69

The European Solidarity Center is strongly associated with the recent history of Gdansk, with the social rebellion of the nation, but also with the construction of ships and the creation of the maritime industry of the post-war period. The architectural concept of the building contains the entire complicated contemporary history of the city. The building is located upon the premises of the shipyard, in a fragment that is no longer part of industrial activities near the Monument of the Fallen Shipyard Workers and Gate No. 2, both significant in the history of the city.

The idea of the architectural concept came about from the memoirs of Wojciech Targowski. When visiting the shipyard, he noted:

> I took a few pictures of the sheet metal for hulls, which were waiting to be used in the manufacturing process, they just stood there leaning on the stands. This was an extremely raw, dynamic message. I still remember the chiaroscuro and the rhythm, which created an almost sculpting form.[52]

The huge structure combines exhibition, research, and education functions. It also houses offices for non-governmental organizations, a library with a reading room, gastronomy, and exhibition spaces.

The monumental architecture of the building has a dynamic, nearly dramatic character. Such a sensation is evoked by the corten finishing of the inclined walls. The interior of the facility is friendly in its character; being a direct opposite of the dynamic form, it creates a spacious, bright space with a large amount of greenery.

Figure 2.8 The European Solidarity Center in Gdansk, PPW Fort Architektura, Wojciech Targowski.
Source: Wojciech Kryński/Fort Targowski.

THE UNIVERSITY OF WARSAW LIBRARY, 1998

ARCHITECTURE:	Marek Budzyński Architect – Partnerzy Marek Budzyński, Krystyna Ilmurzyńska, Zbigniew Badowski
Surface Area:	64,000 m²
Investment Cost:	No data available
Design:	1994
Completion:	1994–1998 (building), 2002 (botanical garden)

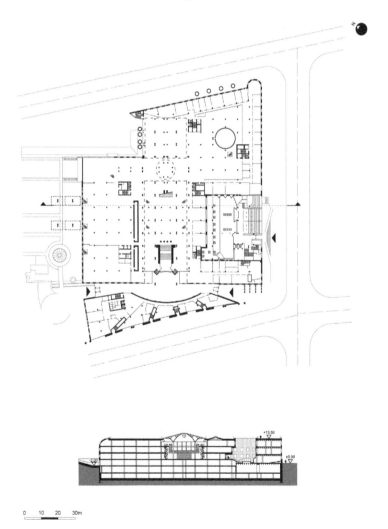

Figure 2.9 The University of Warsaw Library, floor plan and section.
Source: Filip Zamiatnin/book authors.

After the social changes in 1989, some architects began searching for new formal solutions for public utility buildings that would be friendly and useful both to the user and the urban surroundings. The University of Warsaw Library, designed by Marek Budzyński, is a proposal which combines elements of various styles. We see large boards made of patinated copper, which symbolize the pages of books with texts by various authors. Among them, we can find the texts of Jan Kochanowski, Plato, Al-Jahiz, as well as mathematical and musical annotations.

The entrance to the building is found in a passage with a glass roof. Here we find a Latin inscription, *Hic omnia* – "From here everything." The interior of the building is spacious and well-lit with natural light. The rooms have been designed in such a way as to make accessible the extensive book collection while, at the same time, ensuring places for individual work and reading. There are columns by the stairs leading to the first floor, where we see the sculptures of Adam Myjak representing Polish philosophers: Kazimierz Twardowski, Jan Łukasiewicz, Alfred Tarski, and Stanisław Leśniewski. Fragments of their works have been placed as inscriptions upon these columns. The building is distinguished by a green roof, which is used as a place for rest, recreation, and organization of cultural events. Among a varied composition of plants, there are paths, bridges, and pergolas.[53]

It is one of the first public utility buildings of such size that was designed and built after 1989. Here is how Grzegorz Piątek describes it:

> The UWL is more than a building – it is a social phenomenon. It creates a sense of belonging – bonds the academic community with the city inhabitants and tourists. The term "UWLing" was specifically invented to describe sitting in the library simply to hang out with friends.[54]

THE KOSZYKI HALL IN WARSAW, 2016

ARCHITECTURE:	JEMS Architekci – Olgierd Jagiełło, Maciej Miłobędzki, Marcin Sadowski, Jerzy Szczepanik-Dzikowski, Paweł Majkusiak, Mateusz Świętorzecki, and the Medusa Group
Surface Area:	44,849 m²
Investment Cost:	Not available
Design:	2012
Completion:	2016

Figure 2.10 The Koszyki Hall in Warsaw, JEMS Architekci and Medusa Group.
Source: Juliusz Sokołowski/JEMS Architekci.

The Koszyki Hall, also known as the People's Bazaar, was erected in the years 1906–1908 at Koszykowa Street in Warsaw according to the design of Juliusz Dzierżawski in a secessionist style. The name Koszyki (Baskets) probably comes from a rampart that was constructed and strengthened with wicker baskets in the years 1770 and 1771.[55] The hall was demolished in 2009, and only two gatehouses were left standing. The reconstruction of the Koszyki Hall, designed by JEMS Architekci, 2014–2016, took place while maintaining the original fragments of architecture and the commercial function of the structure. As Jerzy-Szczepanik-Dzikowski explained:

> We have designed a modern building, filled with quotes from the past. We are trying to recreate the Hall as best as possible, although what we know about its exterior comes from only two prewar postcards. . . . The most important aspect, is the search for the atmosphere of this place so that today it could be accepted as The Koszyki Hall.[56]

The body of the building had been reconstructed. The arrangements had been rebuilt and renovated, including the preserved secessionist elements of the façade of the gatehouses, the historical trusses, and fragments of the ceramic floors. The characteristic steel construction was exposed in an open space of the hall.[57] The interior is bazaar-like in its character, one in which we can sit down and have a beer or a meal, but one that has been expanded with shops and a bookshop.

The Hall was enlarged with two new wings that house offices. They are architecturally raw and monochromatic in their expression. The rhythm of the narrow windows is in direct contrast to the decorative architecture, fitting perfectly within the frontage of Koszykowa Street.[58] The Medusa Group was also involved in the design works, creating the interiors of the offices along with land development and a system of visual identification.[59]

THE RESTORATION OF CHOPIN PARK IN ŻELAZOWA WOLA, 2010

ARCHITECTURE:	Bolesław Stelmach, Stelmach & Partners Architectural Office
Surface Area:	3,313 m²
Investment Cost:	55.6 M PLN
Design:	2006–2009
Completion:	2008–2010

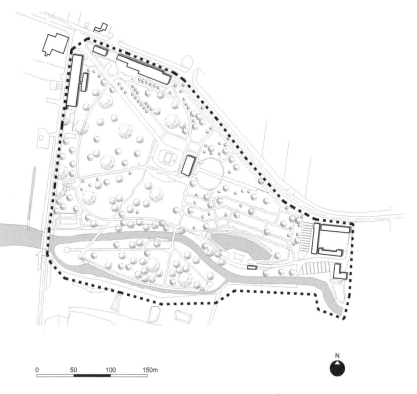

Figure 2.11 Site plan of the restoration of Chopin Park in Żelazowa Wola, Bolesław Stelmach, 2010.

Source: Marta Piórkowska/book authors.

One of the most outstanding examples in which transparent forms of buildings and the selection of materials were taken from the culture of the region is the Fryderyk Chopin Museum in Żelazowa Wola, designed by Bolesław Stelmach.

At the start of the twentieth century, around the old mansion, a modernist park was designed, which later fell into neglect and needed to be restored. The

Value, Beauty, and Place   75

design is a continuation of the original modernist concept of the park. The new pavilions in the park are designed with detail in mind, but also with sensitivity to the tradition of the place, as they bear musical names: the entrance pavilion, along with a multimedia hall and café, is known as "The Prelude," the Étude pavilion houses a multi-functional hall and a restaurant, while the Scherzo is an orangery. The spatial concept of the park is supplemented by open-air elements – a stage with a pond, bridges, and sitting places. Three basic materials were used in the buildings: local stone, wood (Douglas fir), and glass.

The buildings are surrounded by broad glazings, which, depending on the degree of light, are covered with wooden trellises or external blinds. The heavy masonry external walls of the pavilions at the same time make up the wall surrounding the park. On the side of the park, they are nearly completely glazed, opening up onto the greenery that penetrates inside. All these arrangements in various ways open up onto the building of the museum – the old mansion.

In constructing the building, the architects have achieved an atmosphere of relaxation and repose, which is in perfect harmony with the nostalgic atmosphere of the residence.[60] The author intended that the buildings constitute a background for the park and trees, even when we are inside.[61]

The restoration of Żelazowa Wola was awarded a UIA Medal during the UIA Congress in Tokyo in 2011 and was nominated for the Mies van der Rohe Award in 2011.

Figure 2.12 The restoration of Chopin Park in Żelazowa Wola, Bolesław Stelmach, Stelmach & Partners Architectural Office, 2010.

Source: Marcin Czechowicz/Stelmach & Partners Architectural Office.

THE MANUFAKTURA IN ŁÓDŹ, 2006

ARCHITECTURE:	**SHOPPING CENTER, Design:** SUD Architectes, Yannick Pascal, Jean-Marc Pivot
	MS2 MUSEUM OF ART, Design: The Ferdzynowie Design Studio, Bożena I Jacek Ferdzynowie, Biuro Projektów – Jerzy Lutomski
	HOTEL ANDELS, Design: OP Architekten, Wojciech Popławski
Surface Area:	270,000 m²
Investment Cost:	200 M PLN
Design:	1997
Completion:	2002–2006

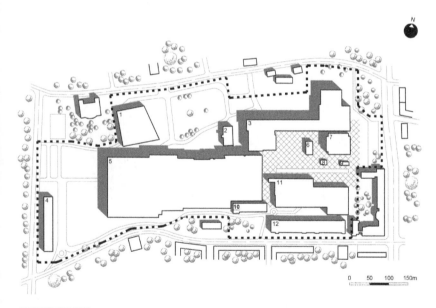

1 PARKING KUBATUROWY
2 SKLEP ZOOLOGICZNY
3 KINO, MUZEUM, STREFA GASTRONOMICZNA, RESTAURACYJNA I REKREACYJNA
4 OBIEKT NIEUŻYTKOWANY
5 GALERIA HANDLOWA
6 KLUB
7 KRĘGIELNIA
8 RESTAURACJA
9 RESTAURACJA
10 MUZEUM MS2
11 RESTAURACJE
12 HOTEL

Figure 2.13 Site plan, the Manufaktura in Łódź.
Source: Filip Zamiatnin/book authors.

Value, Beauty, and Place 77

The Manufaktura Commerce Center has become an important public space in Łódź. The enormous nineteenth-century arrangements contemporarily make up three complexes of buildings: the Manufaktura Shopping Center, the MS² Museum, and the Andels Hotel. All have been established on the remains of a huge factory complex formerly owned by Israel Posnanski, which was created in the second half of the nineteenth century. During Communist times, its ownership was transferred to the state.

In the period of economic transformation, the state-owned plant went bankrupt, while the buildings were taken over by numerous investors. The transformation of the enormous complex into a shopping center began with a decision to preserve the character of its architecture. Brick building elevations, protected by the building conservation officer, were cleared and renovated. The interior of the buildings and halls was modernized and transformed to fit the needs of contemporary commerce. A large, wide 3 ha public space was left between the buildings. It is used for meetings and walks, but also for artistic events. We are reminded of the history of this place by the material, the details, and the historical form of architecture.

As we can see in the present-day description of this location – the previous hard living conditions experienced by the industrial workers have been replaced by a broadly understood "consumerism which is pleasant for the inhabitants."[62]

Figure 2.14 The Manufaktura in Łódź, shopping center designed by SUD Architects, 2006.

Source: Michał Wężowski/Manufaktura, Łódź.

THE KATOWICE CULTURE ZONE, 2015

ARCHITECTURE:	THE SILESIAN MUSEUM – Riegler Riewe Architekten, 2012
	THE NOSPR BUILDING – Tomasz Konior – Konior Studio, 2014
	THE INTERNATIONAL CONGRESS CENTER – JEMS Architekci, 2015
Surface Area:	27.9 ha
Investment Cost:	1 B PLN
Design:	2007
Completion:	2015

During the period of the economic transformation at the end of the twentieth century, Katowice began its own great transformation from an industrial city into a modern European city. On the premises of the nineteenth-century Katowice Mine, shut down in 1999, near the University of Silesia and in the neighborhood of the famous Spodek, the city authorities initiated the creation of the Culture Zone.

Three facilities were completed in this area: the Silesian Museum, by Riegler Riewe Architekten, 2007–2012; the building of the National Symphonic Orchestra of the Polish Radio, by Tomasz Konior, Konior Studio, 2008–2014; and the International Congress Center, by JEMS Architekci, 2008–2015.

The first building of the Culture Zone was the Silesian Museum. The inspiration for its architecture was the mining "subterranean" past of the region, as well as the widespread use of the latest technological achievements. Such thoughts and ideas influenced the concept of locating most of the museum rooms underground, in this way recalling the city's mining past. Glass cuboids were raised above the ground, where entrances, economic and technical facilities, restaurants, ticket offices, etc. are located. The Silesian "glass houses" in the company of an old mining trestle shaft and the restored mining facilities create a landscape in which history intertwines with contemporaneity. The view is especially breathtaking in the evening, when the transparent cuboids illuminate "the place" and the old mining machines.

The NOSPR building, apart from a magnificent concert hall, is also part of the public space of the Culture Zone. Space nearest to the city center contains an entrance square with a fountain and a footbridge built together with the NOSPR building, which is elevated above the level of the square and is also a promenade connecting the city center with university premises. The bridge takes advantage of the differences in terrain in creating a composition that highlights the charm of this place. The area around the building known as the "Katowice Central Park" took on the name of Gardens of the Senses. Around 450 trees and plants of various flowering times were planted. Such arrangements invite guests to use their senses and experience "the spirit of the place," extending the time spent there during all seasons of the year.[63] An added attraction is the Hornbeam Labyrinth, which was inspired by the Plan of Great Katowice from 1926, understood by the designers as a reference to the history of the place, although it is also an allusion to contemporary urban planning.

The nearest to the famous Silesian Spodek is the International Congress Center – an enormous black cuboid as if cut in half. This cut, referred to by architects as a "green canyon," allows visitors to walk on stairs and sidewalks above the building. Visually, it is reminiscent of a green grassy valley of irregular shape, and it is a public space that connects various buildings of the Culture Zone. The attractiveness of the place is further increased by the inclusion of vantage points and an observation deck on top of a grassy hill. The green valley contrasts with and breaks apart the black body of the huge building, creating a possibility to pass above the building along the Zone. The elevations are covered with a black mesh netting which covers up most of the windows, increasing the feeling of uniformity of the body. The black netting was also used inside, where the cutting is clearly visible, marked in the crookedness of the ceiling. The character of the interiors and the dark color schemes bring to mind a mine.

The example of the buildings of the Katowice Culture Zone shows that tradition taken into account in the idea of the design is not opposed to architectural contemporaneity.

The architectural tradition of Silesia, based on experiences of the past, results in "industrial ordinariness" becoming a distinctive feature of the place, creating a formally new quality of architectural beauty.[64] Subsequent investments into the Zone took place as further land plots were accessed and public funds were increased, and as a result, the urban planning of this space may be referred to as "ad hoc urban planning."

The location of the Culture Zone cannot go unmentioned, as it is part of the spatial structure of the Silesian agglomeration. The accessibility of the facilities is influenced both by the leading role of Katowice in the metropolitan system and a quite well-organized transport system. The policy of development of centers of culture and science within the agglomeration which had been shaped for years influenced the uniqueness of the functional combinations contained within the facilities located in the Zone. The diversity, but also the difference of functions, as well as the duration of activities of various kinds influence the attractiveness of "the place."

Figure 2.15 The Culture Zone in Katowice, NOSPR, Tomasz Konior, Konior Studio, 2014; the Silesian Museum, Riegler Riewe Architekten, 2012; the International Congress Center, JEMS Architekci, 2015.

Source: Dominika Werczyńska.

80 *Value, Beauty, and Place*

THE CHURCH OF THE HOLY SPIRIT IN TYCHY, 1982

ARCHITECTURE:	**Stanisław Niemczyk**
Surface Area:	No data available
Completion Cost:	No data available
Design:	Not available
Completion:	1979–1982

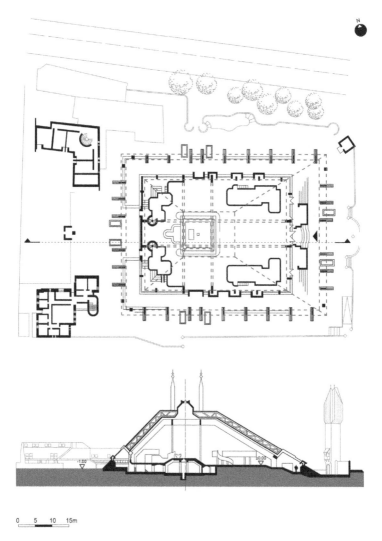

Figure 2.16 The Church of the Holy Spirit in Tychy, floor plan and section.
Source: Marta Piórkowska/book authors.

The Church of the Holy Spirit in Tychy, designed by Stanisław Niemczyk (1943–2019), is an expression of separating oneself from the modernism of the seventies of the twentieth century.

The church in Tychy was the first church designed by the architect. The building was erected between the years 1979 and 1982 far from the city center, in a district which would, in time, be created. Looking at the church from the outside, the most visible is the hipped roof with a skylight and four 12 m high crosses. The roof, which stretches to the ground, brings to mind a tent while also being a reference to the traditional architecture of wooden churches. The bell tower, similarly to an Italian campanile, is placed beside the church building.

The construction of the enormous single-space interior is clearly visible, in the shape of reinforced concrete ribs holding up the tent-like roof. The details of the building, adorned with religious symbols, are also of importance, for instance, door handles in the form of a dove, or symbols imprinted on the floor or the brick walls. The modest wooden interior is distinguished by beautiful polychromies by Jerzy Nowosielski, referencing traditional Byzantine and Christian Orthodox art. Completed in the years 1983–1986[65] with their lively color scheme of the wooden background with warm shades of gold, blue, and red, they make up the beauty of the vast single-space interior. The axis of the building is an altar placed in the center so that it would be illuminated by the natural light coming from the skylight located on the roof. As the creator of this charming and beautiful building said: "The essence of this church is its vertical axis, which connects the earth with heaven."[66]

82 Value, Beauty, and Place
THE HIGHER THEOLOGICAL SEMINARY OF THE RESURRECTIONIST CONGREGATION IN CRACOW, 1996

ARCHITECTURE:	Dariusz Kozłowski, Wacław Stefański, Maria Misiągiewicz
Surface Area:	17,000 m^2
Investment Cost:	No data available
Design:	1984–1992
Completion:	1985–1996

Figure 2.17 The Higher Theological Seminary of the Resurrectionist Congregation in Cracow, Dariusz Kozłowski, Wacław Stefański, Maria Misiągiewicz, 1996.

Source: Dominika Werczyńska.

The Higher Theological Seminary of the Resurrectionist Congregation was designed by Dariusz Kozłowski, Maria Misiągiewicz, and Wacław Stefański. The structure became a part of the canon of Polish architecture as a standard work of postmodernism. Seemingly traditional conventual arrangements with a church, a beautiful refectory, and residential quarters is also an architectural image of a place of worship – a place that creates an atmosphere of mystery, mysticism, and reference to history. Four gates of Initiation, Knowledge, Hope, and Faith lead to understanding the mystery of faith. Each of them is different in form; the best-known is the Gate of Hope, bringing to mind a "tearing," ripping of the reinforced concrete wall. The concrete, according to the words of the creator Dariusz Kozłowski, in the architecture of walls and details fulfills the dream of the transformation of an ordinary object – into a completely different thing, a perfect one. This is especially true of raw poured-in-place concrete:

> [C]oncrete possesses all the traits of the excellence of stone, a building matter acceptable by all; it is the stone of contemporary times. Appropriately prepared it is durable – it is resistant to time. It is also "stone," which can be cast in forms. It is then that it unveils the nobility of the formwork – the smoothness of steel, nature of wood – the concrete casting may take on the form of both skyscraper support as well as a fluted classical column.[67]

The trapezoid courtyard between the buildings opens up onto the view of Twardowski's Rocks Park. The extensive scale of the arrangements – 95,000 m^3 – influences the amount of formal and symbolic aspects of the complex. The designed forms are a reference to the historical elements of sacral and architectural buildings. The architectural forms and details are used in a way that is removed from the functions that are traditionally assigned to them. Frequently, they play a symbolic role, for instance, the two "scenographic" forms located on the roof, relating to a Greek or Eastern place of worship.[68] The entire concept is based on the idea of a historicist axis that can lead from downtown Cracow to Twardowski's Rocks.

The towers, gates, courtyards, portals, and numerous details create the atmosphere and character of this place, similar to the Aldo Rossi Cemetery in Modena.[69] Kozłowski teaches us to ignore the obvious answers and look for our own. He says that the idea of the design "is created from start to finish in the head, in a mysterious, partially unexplored way."[70] The atmosphere of mystery and mysticism clearly confirms the significance of this place.

THE MAŁOPOLSKA GARDEN OF ART IN CRACOW, 2012

ARCHITECTURE:	Ingarden & Ewý Architekci, Architekt Krzysztof Ingarden
Surface Area:	7,116 m²
Investment Cost:	48.2 M PLN
Design:	2005–2008
Completion:	2010–2012

Figure 2.18 The Małopolska Garden of Art in Cracow, Ingarden & Ewý, 2012.
Source: Photo by Krzysztof Ingarden.

The design of the Małopolska Garden of Art by Ingarden & Ewy Architekci is an expansion of the Juliusz Słowacki Theatre and the Voivodship Public Library. Thanks to this investment, the theater acquired two modern theater halls, one for 300 spectators, the other for 80. The library is mainly filled with media of art. Apart from the general resource base for general functions, the facility also houses a bookshop and a café. There is an interesting opening in the roof for a tree that grows out of the library. The height of the building and its dimensions match the scale of the surrounding buildings. The elevation consists of ceramic vertical laths through which the "dropped" cornices pass.

Despite the unusual geometry, which along with the laths creates the drawing of the façade, their height matches the cornices of adjacent buildings.[71] The design of the Małopolska Garden of Art takes into account the character of the location of the new structure and, despite the non-conventional architectural beauty, fits exceptionally well into the historical center of Cracow. This uncommon building is located among nineteenth-century houses. The architecture blurs the boundaries between the interior and the surroundings, only upon a closer look it becomes apparent that the urban "envelope" or "skin" of the building does not constitute a house. It creates the edge of a "secret garden" hidden in the city tissue.

In some circles, the building and the context are perceived as Cracow's Centre Pompidou. The architecture seems to be a combination of new technologies with a nostalgic atmosphere of a small town, but also of Cracow from the period of artistic Polish Bohemianism. The function, in combination with the characteristic architecture of the building, clearly elevates the value of perception of the building and results in it becoming an exceptional place.

Notes

1 J. Otterbeck (ed.), *Oslo Opera House*, Oslo 2009, p. 44 and A. Radford, S. Morkoç, A. Srivastava, *The Elements of Modern Architecture. Understanding Contemporary Buildings*, Warsaw 2017, pp. 318–323.
2 J. Otterbeck (ed.), *Oslo Opera House* . . ..
3 Ibid.
4 Ibid.
5 . R Venturi, D. Brown Scott, A. Tamas, *Interview: Robert Venturi & Denise Brown Scott, by Andrea Tamas*, interviewed by S. Jordana, www.archdaily.com/130389/interview-robert-venturi-denise-scott-brown-by-andrea-tamas [access: 27.05.2021].
6 Mapel, *Muzeum z pudełek*, www.bryla.pl/bryła/1,85298,464640,muzeum-z-pudełek.html [access: 27.05.2021] and also N. Juzwa, "My" Houses In New York. Appearance, Utility, Originality, in: *Czasopismo Techniczne*, ed. D. Kozłowski, Cracow 2016, pp. 61–73.
7 Ibid.
8 R. Peltason, G. Ong-Yan (ed.), *Architect. Pritzker Prize Laureates in their own Words Architect*, London 2010, pp. 10–15.
9 *OMA rozbuduje Muzeum Sztuki Współczesnej w Nowym Jorku*, www.bryla.pl/bryła/7,85298,2497855,oma-rozbudowuje-nowe-muzeum-sztuki-wspolczesnej-w-nowym-jorku [access: 27.05.2021].
10 The IBA Program was connected with the European REKULA Project Interreg GIIIB Cases, in which three groups participated: Italy: Regional Administration of Veneto a. Fondazione Benetton Studi Ricerche; Poland: Silesian University of Technology; Germany, the leaders of the project from the IBA Foundation, Lower Lusatia. Prof. N. Juzwa was the leader of the Polish group and the co-author of the text.
11 The artist Peter Kuhn from Berlin, who designed the lighting in the F60 project, cooperated with Rolf Kuhn.
12 See. T. Kozłowski, *Architektura a sztuka*, Cracow 2018.
13 Le Corbusier, "*W stronę architektury*, transl. by T. Swoboda, Warsaw 2012, p. 80.
14 A. Basista, *Wartość i architektura*, Cracow 2005.
15 N. Juzwa (ed.), *Architektura* . . ..
16 T. Dyckhoff, *The Age of Spectacle* . . ., p. 20.

86 *Value, Beauty, and Place*

17 H. Jahn, *Popchnąć świat do przodu – Helmut Jahn i jego klasyczny modernizm*, interviewed by M. Mróz, https://internityhome.pl/ih4/popchnac-swiat-przodu-helmut-jahn-klasyczny-modernizm/ [access: 27.05.2021].
18 Z. Paszkowski, *Ponadczasowa wartość architektury*, "Czasopismo techniczne" Cracow 2011, vol. 108, pp. 300–304.
19 This was the topic of the month for the monthly Znak titled *In Search of Beauty*, which was announced by Dürer's quote, pp. 4i 11. Questions about beauty are responded to by Semir Zeki, Anna Arno, Zygmunt Bauman, Anda Rottenberg, monthly. Znak, no. 736, 9/2016, pp. 4–31.
20 S. Zeki, Beauty Is the Most Important Thing, Znak, no. 736, 9/2016, pp. 6–11.
21 Z. Baumann, Jak Galatea Narcyzem się stała, Znak, no. 736, 9/2016, pp. 18–23.
22 A title was used here op. cit.
23 Ibid. S. Zeki, *Piękno . . .*, p. 8.
24 Ibid.
25 Ibid, A. Rottenberg, *Należy sobie zaufać*, pp. 24–31.
26 Ibid.
27 W. Tatarkiewicz, *O doskonałości*, Warsaw 1976, pp. 42–56.
28 See: P. Węcławik, *Antropologia filozoficzna Maxa Schelera. Jej geneza, przedmiot i metoda*, "Folia Philosophica" 1998, vol. 16, pp. 103–113.
29 Roman Ingarden, O dziele architektury, in: *Studia z estetyki*, vol. 2, Warsaw 1966.
30 cf. Ch. Jencks.
31 W. Tatarkiewicz, *Dzieje sześciu pojęć*, Warsaw 1975, p. 137 and ff.
32 See: D. Dutton, *The Art of Instinct . . .*, p. 315.
33 Ibid., p. 316.
34 P. Goldberger, *Swiss Mystique*, www.vanity fair.com/peter-zumthor-architect-buildings [access: 28.05.2021].
35 R. Ingarden, O dziele architektury, in: *Studia z estetyki*, Warsaw 1958, pp. 115–116.
36 Ibid.
37 The large number of buildings created in Silesia is, in a way, a subjective choice of the authors. However, of equal importance is the noticeable many years of negligence of the region/industrial city, "the mediocrity" of the city environment, as well as the clearly visible change in recent years. This fact seems noteworthy.
38 The main theses of a conference titled "Defining Architectural Space," *Faculty of Architecture of the Cracow University of Technology*, Cracow 2019.
39 P. Zumthor, *Personal Interview with Edward Lifson for His Blog*, architecturalinterviews.blogspot.com/2009/12/peter-zumthor-personal-interview-with.html [access: 27.05.2021].
40 Space is "an unlimited three-dimensional area, in which all physical phenomena occur," according to a definition from the PWN Polish Dictionary https://sjp.pwn.pl/sip/przestrzen;25112511283.html [access: 27.05.2021].
41 Y.F. Tuan, *Space and Place*, transl. by. A. Morawińska, Warsaw 1987.
42 B. Jałowiecki, *Miejsce, przestrzeń, obszar*, "Przegląd Socjologiczny" 2011, no. 60.
43 M. Stangel, *Cities for People – an Interview with Jan Gehl*, http://arcastangel.pl/miasta-dla-ludzi-rozmowa-z-janem-gehlem/ [access: 2.02.2020].
44 E.P. Porębska, Polska na mapie architektury, in: *Form Follows Freedom. Architektura dla kultury w Polsce 2000*, eds. J. Purchla, J. Sepioł, Cracow 2015, p. 46.
45 T. Dyckhoff, *The Age Spectacle . . .*, pp. 106–128.
46 J. Gehl, *Life Between Buildings*, transl. by M.A. Urbańska, Cracow 2009, p. 177.
47 Ibid.
48 *Center for the Meeting of Cultures. History*, www.spotkaniakultur.com/index.php/pl/o-csk [access: 18. 11.2019].
49 Ibid.

50 Center for the Meeting of Cultures in Lublin, https://architektura.info/architektura/polska_i_swiat/centrum_spotkania_kultur_w_lublinie [access: 28.05.2021].
51 Center for the Meeting of Cultures, https://culture.pl/pl/dzielo/centrum-spotkania-kultur [access: 28.05.2021] and T. Michalak, *Teatr Otwarty*, "Architektura-Murator" 2016, no. 8, pp. 64–65.
52 *The European Solidarity Center*, www.bryla.pl/bryla/1,85301,16504373,Europejskie-Centrum-Solidarności-w-Gdansku-ZDJECIA [access: 28.05.2021].
53 *The Warsaw University Library, Building, and Garden*, www.buw.uw.edu.pl/o-nas/budynek-i-ogrod/ [access: 28.05.2021].
54 G. Piątek, *Co architektura mówi o Polakach*, http://wyborcza.pl/1,75410,16742445,Co_architektura_mowi_o_Polakach.html [access: 28.05.2021].
55 The location of the rampart had, until the twentieth century, functioned as the border of the city.
56 See: R. Geremek, *Koszyki pełne historii*, Warsaw 2014, pp. 4–5, 60–65 (pdf), pp. 62–63.
57 *The Koszyki Hall*, http://jems.pl/projekty/wszystkie-prace/hala-koszyki.html [access: 28.05.2021] and R. Geremek, *Koszyki pełne...*, pp. 4–5, 60–65 (pdf).
58 *The Koszyki Hall*, http://jems.pl/projekty/wszystkie-prace/hala-koszyki.htm [access: 28.05.2021].
59 *The Koszyki Halli*, www.medusagroup.pl/projekty/handlowe/hala-koszyki-2/ [access: 28.05.2021].
60 N. Juzwa, A. Gil, K. Ujma-Wąsowicz, *Almost Human Architecture*, http://kaiu.pan.pl/index.php?option=com_content&view=article&id=463&catid=60&Itemid=56 [access: 328.05.2021].
61 B. Stelmach, *Dotyk ciszy. O rewaloryzacji Parku Pomnika w miejscowości urodzenia Fryderyka Chopina w żelazowej Woli/The touch of silence. Restoration of the Park Monument in the Birthplace of Frederic Chopin – Żelazowa Wola*, transl. by J. Lampla, Lublin 2014.
62 A. Cymer, *Łódzkie fabryki wczoraj i dziś*, culture.pl/pl/artykul/lodzkie-fabryki-wczoraj-i-dzis [access: 28.05.2021] and *Manufaktura, Rewitalizacja*, www.manufaktura.com/site/479/powstanie-manufaktury/rewitalizacja [access: 28.05.2021].
63 T. Malkowski, M. Szczelina, (ed.), *Dotknąć muzyki*, Katowice 2014 and T. Konior, *Ewolucja przestrzeni publicznej*, Ph.D. dissertation, The Lodz University of Technology 2019.
64 J. Świerzawski, Przemiana, in: *Tożsamość. 100 lat polskiej architektury*, eds. B. Stelmach, K. Batko-Andrzejewska, Warsaw 2019.
65 P. Oczko, *Tychy. Sacrum w mieście socjalistycznym*, Tychy 2019, p. 62 and B. Kopia, *Muzeum Miejskie w Tychach*, http://muzeum.tychy.pl/zbiory/fotografia/zygmunt-wieczorek/ [access: 28.05.2021].
66 S. Niemczyk, *Krajobraz pierwotny. An interview with Stanisław Niemczyk*, "Architektura i Biznes" 2002, no. 12, p. 34, see: P. Oczko, *Tychy. Sacrum...*, p. 62.
67 D. Kozłowski, *Beton i mistrzowie transmutacji materii*, "Pretekst" 2018, no. 8, p. 70.
68 B. Stec, *Wyższe Seminarium Duchowne Księży Zmartwychwstańców Centrum Ressurectionist*, https://pomoszlak.pl/seminarium-zmartwychwstancow/ [access: 28.05.2021].
69 Ibid.
70 Text based on: P. Pięciak, *W świecie fikcji, opery, wspaniałego kłamstwa i betonu*, https//architekturabetonowa.pl/aktualności/1257/wswiecie-fikcji-opery-wspanialego-klamstwa-i-betonu/ [access: 28.05.2021].
71 N. Juzwa, A. Gil, K. Ujma-Wasowicz, *Almost Human*... and K. Ingarden, *Założenia autorskie*, "Architektura-Murator" 2013, no. 1 (220), pp. 44–45.

Part III Presentation of Polish Examples

Introduction

The political, social, and technical changes at the end of the twentieth and the beginning of the twenty-first centuries significantly influenced the shape of Polish architecture. The transformation of the economy, Poland's access into the European Union, and the benefits connected with it stemming from the possibility to take advantage of European funds changed the ways that projects were financed, especially in public utility architecture. The progressing digitalization of the architect's profession and the opening up of Poland and Polish designers onto the world changed the attitudes towards architecture as well as many of the principles shaping architecture and the profession.

As a result, numerous beautiful and sometimes noteworthy building were completed, which, although still are striving to catch up with modern technology, are able to successfully compete with the world because of their concept and architectural beauty.

As we have promised, the buildings presented were completed between 1980 and 2018. Information regarding the buildings presented in the book was obtained from designers and building users, as well as from literature and professional magazines, such as *Architektura-Murator* or *Architektura i Biznes*. Drawings of floor plans and sections of the buildings have been developed specifically for the purposes of the book. The examples are presented, separated by functions, meaning, the content of the interior and also based on the time of building completion.

POLISH ARCHITECTURE – EXAMPLES
OFFICE BUILDINGS

The Focus in Warsaw
The Social Insurance Building in Zabrze
The Warsaw Stock Exchange
The BRE Bank (now mBank) in Bydgoszcz
The Agora Offices in Warsaw
The Zana House in Lublin
The Science and Technology Park in Lublin
The Q22 in Warsaw
The Baltic in Poznan

Presentation of Polish Examples 89

COURTHOUSES

The Supreme Court in Warsaw
The District Court in Katowice

MUSEUMS

The Cricoteka Center for the Documentation of the Art of Tadeusz Kantor in Cracow
The Porta Posnania ICHOT in Poznan
The World War II Museum in Gdansk
The European Solidarity Center in Gdansk *Description in Part 2*
Restoration of the Chopin Park in Żelazowa Wola *Description in Part 2*
The Silesian Museum *Description in Part 2*
The POLIN Museum of the History of Polish Jews in *Description in Part 1*
Warsaw

CULTURAL FACILITIES

The Chopin Center in Warsaw
The Służewski House of Culture in Warsaw
The Shakespeare Theatre in Gdansk
The Center for the Meeting of Cultures in Lublin *Description in Part 2*
The Małopolska Garden of Art in Cracow *Description in Part 2*
The International Congress Center in Katowice *Description in Part 2*

HOUSES OF MUSIC

The Krzysztof Penderecki European Music Center in Lusławice
The "Symfonia" Center of Musical Science and Education in Katowice
The Podlaska Opera in Białystok
The Mieczysław Karłowicz Philharmonic in Szczecin
The Jordanki Cultural and Congress Center in Torun
The Building of the National Symphonic Orchestra of the *Description in*
Polish Radio in Katowice *Part 1 and Part 2*

SPORTS FACILITIES

The Flyspot in Mory, near Warsaw

EDUCATIONAL FACILITIES

The Copernicus Science Center in Warsaw
The Finance Faculty of the University of Economics in Cracow
The Białołęka Middle School and Cultural Center
The Faculty of Neophilology and Applied Linguistics of the University of Warsaw in
Warsaw
The Krzysztof Kieślowski Film School of the University of Silesia

LIBRARIES

The Center of Academic Information and the Academic
Library in Katowice
The Raczyński Library in Poznan
The University of Warsaw Library *Description in Part 2*

CHURCHES

The Church of the Ascension of the Lord in Warsaw
The Votum Aleksa
The Church of the Holy Spirit in Tychy *Description in Part 2*
The Higher Theological Seminary of the Resurrectionist
   Congregation in Cracow *Description in Part 2*

COMMERCE

The Koszyki Hall in Warsaw *Description in Part 2*
The Manufaktura in Łódź *Description in Part 2*

OFFICE BUILDINGS

92 Presentation of Polish Examples

THE FOCUS IN WARSAW, 2001

ARCHITECTURE: Kuryłowicz & Associates
Surface Area: 64,000 m^2
Investment Cost: No data available
Design: 1997–1998
Completion: 1997–2001

Figure 3.1 The Focus building in Warsaw, Kuryłowicz & Associates, 2001.
Source: Wojciech Kryński/Apaka.

The Focus office building, by Stefan Kuryłowicz (1949–2011), is situated in downtown Warsaw, near a park, surrounded by high office buildings, dormitories, and residential houses. The building was designed on a plan of a square (67.00 × 65.50 m), and with a height of nearly 49 m.[1]

The main entrance, which is announced by an enormous "urban window" on the elevation, leads to a glazed courtyard, around which the functional structure of the interior is centered. The service and commerce facilities are located on the ground and first floor, the office rooms above. The three underground stories house a multi-level parking lot.

Functionally, the building is divided into four parts, which are accessed by vertical cores placed in the corners of the inner courtyard. On the sixth story from the south side, there is a four-story winter garden. The authors put a lot of emphasis on details as well as individually designed elements of building equipment, such as stairs, elevators, and others.[2]

The building is in line with European standards of office architecture. This is expressed by the words of Wojciech Laskowski: "the enormous space of this atrium, so precisely designed, has no equal in Polish post-war architecture."[3] Even after many years, these words still sound convincing.

The southern elevation is a two-layered glass partition with blinds, which are electrically controlled. The eastern and western elevations are finished off with black polished granite, while the two highest stories are covered with titanium zinc alloy-plated sheet steel, highlighted by a protruding cornice in the shape of an airplane wing. The design was distinguished in 2001 during the Association of Polish Architects (Stowarzyszenie Architektów Polskich – SARP) Awards, where it received the main award – the Polish Cement in Architecture.

THE SOCIAL INSURANCE BUILDING IN ZABRZE, 1997

ARCHITECTURE: Inarko, Andrzej Duda and Henryk Zubel
Surface Area: 11,400 m^2
Investment Cost: No data available
Design: 1992–1994
Completion: 1994–1997

Figure 3.2 The Social Insurance Building in Zabrze, Inarko, Andrzej Duda and Henryk Zubel, 1997.

Source: Dominika Werczyńska.

The Social Insurance Building in Zabrze, by Andrzej Duda and Henryk Zubel, was created in the years 1994–1997. It is situated in the city center, near nineteenth-century buildings. The authors of the ZUS Building relating to industrial heritage present a good example of inner-city Silesian architecture. The brick building with glazed two lower stories and rhythmically spaced-out windows matches the height of the other buildings and the regulation line of the street. The simplicity of the elevation is also characterized by the finishing of the interior, which is concentrated around two corridors that are parallel to the street. The layout allows for the rooms inside the building to be well lit. One of the courtyards has a glazed roof – it is the location of the main customer service desk.

The ZUS office in Zabrze is distinct with modesty of form, consistently repeated in the type of material used. The concept of restrained architecture was praised by the academic community as well as the Silesian architectural community.[4] The building was awarded first prize of the Silesian Voivode (1998), as well as the SARP Award (1998), and finally, first prize of the Minister of Internal Affairs and Administration (1999).

THE WARSAW STOCK EXCHANGE, 2000

ARCHITECTURE:	Stanisław Fiszer, Andrzej M. Chołdzyński
Floor Space:	~29,000 m²
Investment Cost:	No data available
Design:	1994–2000
Completion:	1998–2000

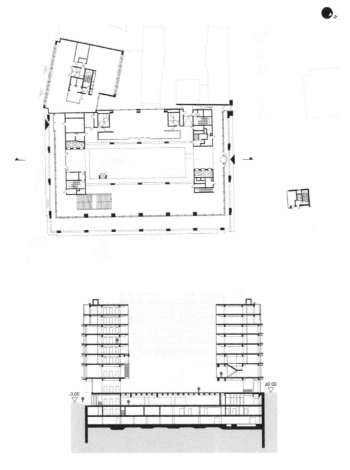

Figure 3.3 The Warsaw Stock Exchange, floor plan and section.
Source: Paulina Nagel/book authors.

Opened in the year 2000, the Warsaw Stock Exchange Building, by Stanisław Fiszer and Andrzej M. Chołdzyński, is situated in an area filled with tenement houses built prior to World War I. The building is distinguished by extensive glazings of the elevation as well as the use of decoration and details, which are characterized by a modern formal expression. For example, cast aluminum castings adorned with symbolic charts and recordings of stock market quotations. The stone parts are also decorated with inscription and diverse texture.

The exterior of the building suggests its content, meaning, the transparency of a financial institution. Several 40 m escalators lead to the third floor, situated in a glazed hall, and seem to be a symbol of economic growth. They are supplemented by a formally exquisite spiral steel and glass stairs for brokers.[5]

The so-called floor, which plays a representative role here, is a reference to the history of world stock exchange. In the past, all the financial transactions took place there, but today they are completed with the use of IT systems.

The structure was nominated for the Mies van der Rohe Award in 2001.

THE BRE BANK (NOW MBANK) IN BYDGOSZCZ, 2000

ARCHITECTURE:	BIM – Bulanda I Mucha Architekci
Surface Area:	4,755 m^2
Investment Cost:	No data available
Design:	1994
Completion:	2000

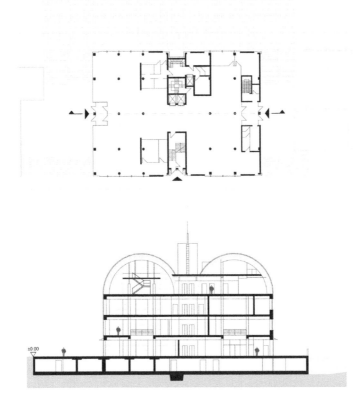

Figure 3.4 The BRE Bank, floor plan and section.
Source: Paulina Nagel/book authors.

The BRE Bank building in Bydgoszcz, present-day mBank, by BiM – Andrzej Bulanda and Włodzimierz Mucha (1956–2019) – was the first building completed after 1989, which became an icon of Polish architecture. In the words of its author Andrzej Bulanda, the building

> is an attempt to find the simplest gesture to complete the Brda waterfront in the historical center of Bydgoszcz. An old granary, a symbol of the place was selected as the typological form. It was contemporarily processed while maintaining the scale of its surroundings.[6]

In its form, the building relates to historical granaries, illustrating the function of the bank as a granary for money. Two geometrically similarly shaped four-story bodies differ from each other by the material used to finish the elevation. One is glass and transparent, like an ideal financial institution; the other brick, symbolizing durability and safety of this contemporary treasure chest. Here is what the authors had to say:

> We are an architectural design studio, designing contemporary architecture with strong ties to the context of the place. . . . This design came from the need to respect the unprecedented atmosphere of the city waterfront. It was about highlighting . . . that specific genius loci of the waterfront and the nearby harbor.[7]

The surface of the terrace around the building is a waterfront public space with a beautiful wooden floor, resting places, and a view of the river. Important features of this architecture include form referencing the history of the place and conscious diversification of materials.

The building received numerous distinctions and awards. The most important are the Annual SARP Award in 2000 and a nomination to the Mies van der Rohe Award in 2001. Andrzej Bulanda and Włodzimierz Mucha were awarded the Honorary SARP Award in 2015.

THE AGORA OFFICES IN WARSAW, 2001

ARCHITECTURE:	JEMS Architekci – Olgierd Jagiełło, Maciej Miłobędzki, Marcin Sadowski, Jerzy Szczepanik-Dzikowski
Surface Area:	36,896 m^2
Investment Cost:	140 M PLN
Design:	1998
Completion:	2000–2001

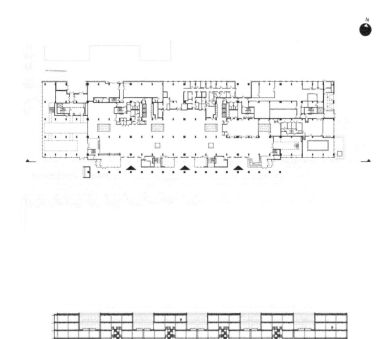

Figure 3.5 The Agora Offices, floor plan and section.
Source: Paulina Nagel/book authors.

The Agora Offices, office building by JEMS Architekci, is situated outside the Warsaw city center. Glazed, diversely shaped elevations reflect the transparent character of the institution. A characteristic feature of the architecture are wooden razors mounted on steel construction on the southern elevation.

The structure and the functional solutions of the building are uniform in character. The construction, interior divisions, solutions used in office and general-access interiors, as well as the room solutions are integrally designed.

The interior of the building is open in its character. Transparent glass dividing walls and atriums which run through every floor of the building create a single-space character of the interiors and form the character not only of each floor but of the whole building itself as well. Appropriate use of finishing materials – wood, glass, concrete, and steel – in combination with greenery and skillfully designed extra lighting with natural and artificial light creates a friendly atmosphere of the interior.[8]

The design and building completion were awarded the Prize of the Minister of Infrastructure for the design team and the Best Building in Warsaw Award in the years 2002–2003 in a competition titled "Life in Architecture," organized by the monthly *Architektura-Murator*.

THE ZANA HOUSE IN LUBLIN, 2008

ARCHITECTURE:	Bolesław Stelmach, Stelmach & Partners Architectural Office
Surface Area:	1,320 m^2
Investment Cost:	No data available
Design:	2005–2006
Completion:	2008

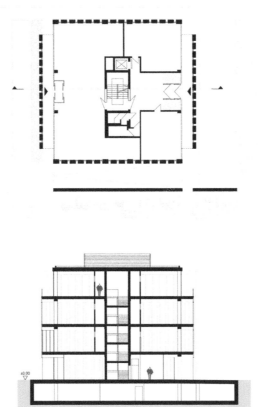

Figure 3.6 The Zana House Offices, floor plan and section.
Source: Paulina Nagel/book authors.

The Zana House Office Building in Lublin, designed by the Bolesław Stelmach design studio, was erected among unordered architecture made up of residential buildings and nearby supermarkets. In the words of the architect, Bolesław Stelmach:

> The context is a hostile, spatial chaos, accidental, ugly buildings without any green areas. Therefore, it was necessary to draw a house which would completely negate its surroundings. A house which would justify itself with its structure and elevations directed inwards. It is a silent house – the only plausible response to such a context.[9]

In accordance with that idea, the Zana House boasts a simple form reminiscent of a cube. The elevations create a rhythm of vertical concrete elements, behind which windows are located. In opposition to most contemporary office buildings, from the outside the building seems closed. The vertical concrete divisions of elevations, the finishing, and the diligently crafted details create a sensation that the architecture apparently hides a high-ranking function.

The structure of the building is transparent and clear – the building cores, along with the reinforced concrete elements of the elevation, fulfill load-bearing functions. There are open-space offices organized around the core. The last story houses a bar and green terraces.[10] The structure was distinguished in a SARP competition in a category of buildings completed using private funds in 2008[11] and was also finalist of the 2012 edition of the "Life in Architecture" competition.

THE SCIENCE AND TECHNOLOGY PARK IN LUBLIN 2014

ARCHITECTURE: Bolesław Stelmach, Stelmach & Partners Architectural Office
Surface Area: 7,490 m²
Investment Cost: No data available
Design: 2003–2004
Completion: 2014

Figure 3.7 The Science and Technology Park in Lublin, Bolesław Stelmach, Stelmach & Partners Architectural Office, 2014, floor plan and section.

Source: Marcin Czechowicz/Stelmach & Partners Architectural Office.

The Science and Technology Park Building, designed by Bolesław Stelmach, is situated near downtown Lublin. When in a competition organized in 2003 the winning design was announced, the area only included several scattered buildings. The park was to become the commencement of development and order of a new, nascent economic zone.[12]

The mission of the Lublin Science and Technology Park was to "support the development of the Lublin Voivodeship by creating a platform for the cooperation of Lublin universities as well as business representatives and the start-up community."[13] Today the building has become a place for meetings between the academic and business communities. The modest, clear structure of the body consists of five concrete modules of various functions that match the decline of the terrain. The simple, cubic forms with a vertical window rhythm have bright interiors, thanks to roof skylights and internal gardens. The core appropriately connects different functions, which are situated in subsequent "modules." The first houses innovation and implementation laboratories and training rooms. The second contains linked multi-function rooms. The main entrance is located in the central module along with the exhibition space, a café, and the reception desk. The two final modules contain an innovation incubator, in which Lublin universities function.

The dominant features of the architecture are architectural concrete and glass as well as elements of black steel and oak. Details made out of concrete and wood create a positive internal atmosphere.[14]

THE Q22 IN WARSAW, 2016

ARCHITECTURE: Kuryłowicz & Associates
Floor Space: 89,273 m^2
Investment Cost: 500 M PLN
Design: 2010–2013
Completion: 2016

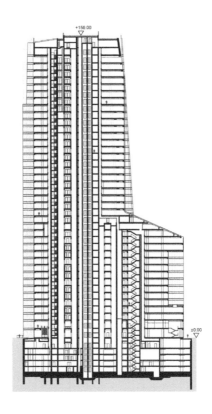

Figure 3.8 The O22 Offices in Warsaw, floor plan and section.
Source: Paulina Nagel/book authors.

The immense 155 m high office building the Q22, designed by Kuryłowicz & Associates, was created on the premises of the old Mercury Hotel.

The building consist of two wings; the side, lower wing of the Q22 consists of 15 stories whose height matches the nearby buildings. Research was undertaken as far as the shape and height of the higher building to check visibility. A response was a form that is reminiscent of a huge glass crystal. The entrance and services which are on the ground floor are delicately accentuated on the elevations thanks to divisions of the glazing which indicate diversity of functions. The vertical transport system is an arrangement of two unconnected lift cabins located in a single shaft. The inclined glass roof is equipped with photovoltaic installations, thus generating energy for charging electric vehicles. Apart from 50,000 m² of office space, the building contains conference rooms, restaurants, as well as gyms.[15]

The authors of the skyscraper were distinguished in 2019 in a competition for the Prize of the Minister of Investment and Economic Development for outstanding creative achievements in the fields of architecture, civil engineering, and spatial planning and development. The skyscraper was also nominated for the Body of the Year Award in 2016 (tn. pl. Bryła Roku).

THE BALTIC IN POZNAN, 2017

ARCHITECTURE:	MVRDV, NO – Natkaniec, Olechnicki Architekci
Surface Area:	25,000 m²
Investment Cost:	150 M PLN
Design:	since 2008
Completion:	2014–2017

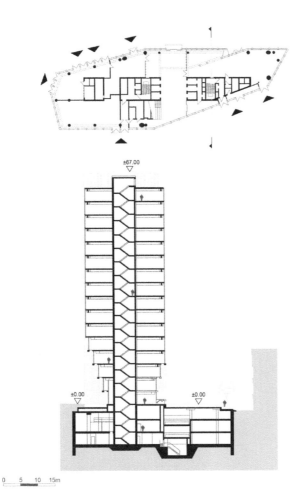

Figure 3.9 The Baltic in Poznań, floor plan and section.
Source: Paulina Nagel/book authors.

The Poznan-based 16-story office building the Baltic, by the Dutch MVRDV company, in cooperation with NO – Natkaniec, Olechnicki Architekci – is situated near the Poznan International Fairgrounds. Thanks to cuts placed in cascades, the building looks different from every side; the outline of the body extends or narrows depending on where it is viewed from.

The architects were inspired by another well-known Poznan building, the *Okrąglak*, designed by Marek Leykam. The motif of windows placed in distinct frames, which was also repeated in the building elevations, was directly inspired by Leykam's work. The elevation consists of vertical and horizontal delicate, prefabricated concrete elements. Beneath the external structure, whose materiality is reminiscent of stone, hides an aluminum construction.

The stepped arrangement of form allows for additional lighting of the interior as well as the creation of terraces with a view of the city. Moving back, the corner of the enormous body from the side of the Kaponiera Roundabout emphasizes the entrance, while the retraction from the side of the old printing house allows for opening up the interiors to the panorama of the city. Besides business functions, the two lower stories contain shops, a hotel, restaurants, a gym, and a small jazz club on the 16th floor.[16] The construction of the building is made of reinforced concrete, and it is created by columns and ceilings connected with a vertical core. The remaining elements of the construction are made out of steel.[17]

The building was the laureate of the Jan Baptysta Quadro Award[18] for best building in the city in 2017.

COURTHOUSES

112 *Presentation of Polish Examples*

THE SUPREME COURT IN WARSAW, 1999

ARCHITECTURE:	Marek Budzyński, Zbigniew Badowski
Surface Area:	44,744 m²
Investment Cost:	~300 M PLN
Design:	1991
Completion:	1999

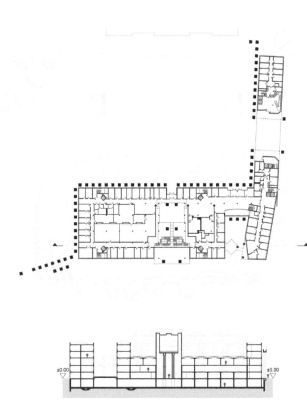

Figure 3.10 The Supreme Court in Warsaw, floor plan and section.
Source: Paulina Nagel/book authors.

The competition for the new building of the Supreme Court in Warsaw was won in 1991 by Marek Budzyński and Zbigniew Badowski. The elevations of the great building, made out of greenish, reflective glass, underline the transparency of the institution. They were concealed with a colonnade, whose symbolism is expressed in a rhythm of 76 columns finished off with patinated copper sheet metal. The columns contain 76 inscriptions from Roman law which are inscribed in Polish and Latin.

The glass and patinated copper of the colonnade create a dignified character of a large building. The material was selected in such a way in order to reference the patinated roofs and domes of other Warsaw buildings.[19] The capitols of the columns are adorned with the motif of a scale, attributed to the Titaness of Divine Law and Order, Themis, and on the top of each column there is a different plant. The columns by the Warsaw Uprising monument are adorned with the emblem of the Polish Underground State. The architects call this rhythm of columns "a colonnade of law." It symbolizes the rhythm of the law, which governs the rhythm of life. The plants on the columns are, for the designers, an architectural detail that conveys "unity of Culture and Nature."[20] There are three sculptures on the courtyard at the back of the building: *Faith*, *Hope*, and *Love*. The immense, full-of-various-stories-and-symbols building is an example of contemporary storytelling architecture. The dominant material in the interior is glass. Most of the nine courtrooms are provided additional lighting with natural light.[21]

The Supreme Court was the first new building for the authorities of the Third Republic of Poland, and its symbolism aroused emotions. The building was praised as an exceptional work of architecture but was also described as frivolous and "unreal."[22]

For the completion of the Supreme Court building, Marek Budzyński received the main prize, the Polish Cement in Architecture 2000, as well as the first prize of the Minister of Infrastructure in 2004.

THE DISTRICT COURT IN KATOWICE, 2009

ARCHITECTURE:	Archistudio Studniarek + Pilinkiewicz
Surface Area:	15,500 m^2
Investment Cost:	50 M PLN
Design:	2003–2004
Completion:	2005–2009

Figure 3.11 The District Court in Katowice, Archistudio Studniarek + Pilinkiewicz, 2009.
Source: Dominika Werczyńska.

The District Court in Katowice, by Archistudio Studniarek + Pilinkiewicz, is situated on the outskirts of the city center. The Archistudio design studio won a competition in 2003 designing a building which is an element that links but also closes off a quarter of city buildings.

The building, situated along the east–west axis, has two wings, a northern one and a southern one, which are connected via a hallway on the ground floor and via internal courtyards and vertical cores at higher stories. As a result, a long rectangular building was created, whose monumental architecture highlights its function. The main entrance with a staircase, along the long axis of the building, is a large portal with columns supporting the roof. An accent of the entrance façade is a protruding cuboid that houses the courtroom. The high, accentuated-by-columns entrance into the building arouses respect and underlines the street frontage. Simple, almost-monotonous long walls, with a uniform rhythm of windows, are set in sandy clinker and seem to an even greater degree highlight the importance of the functions of the interior. The second entrance on the opposite side of the building is more sculpted.

The structure has 51 hearing rooms and over 600 other rooms.[23] The hallway on the ground floor serves transport purposes and has natural light thanks to the courtyard. The raw character of the simply shaped body is alleviated by wooden construction of the glass façade. The building fills an urban gap between the modern buildings in Katowice, which were erected here in the year 2000. It was nominated for the Mies van der Rohe Award in 2011, and it won first prize in a SARP competition – the Polish Cement in Architecture 2010 – as well as in Competition for the Best Public Space of the Silesian Voivodeship 2010.

MUSEUMS

THE CRICOTEKA CENTER FOR THE DOCUMENTATION OF THE ART OF TADEUSZ KANTOR IN CRACOW, 2014

ARCHITECTURE:	nsMoonstudio – Piotr Nawara and Agnieszka Szultk and the Wizja Stanisław Deńko Design Studio
Surface Area:	5,342 m²
Investment Cost:	50 M PLN
Design:	2006
Completion:	2010–2014

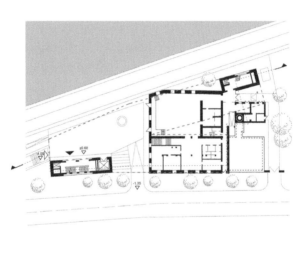

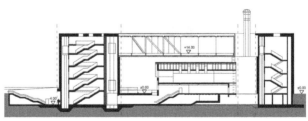

Figure 3.12 The Cricoteca in Cracow, floor plan and section.

Source: Filip Zamiatnin/book authors.

The Cricoteka began its activities in 1980 in Cracow. The man behind this project was Tadeusz Kantor, who created the Cricoteka Cricot 2 Theatre Center. After his death, the name was changed to the Cricoteka Center for the Documentation of the Art of Tadeusz Kantor.

The residence of the Cricoteka Center for the Documentation of the Art of Tadeusz Kantor, 2014, designed by Stanisław Deńko, Piotr Nawara, and Agnieszka Szultk, was erected on the premises of a former electric power plant. In an original way, the architects adapted the existing post-industrial buildings. They placed the large body standing on "two feet" and a support above the buildings.[24] The inspiration for such a design was a drawing made by Tadeusz Kantor depicting a man carrying a table.[25]

The body of the building, which is 20 m high and 83.5 m long, is finished with panels made out of corten in which small openings were cut out. Standing in front of the building, one can see the mirror bottom of the building out of steel sheet, in which the Vistula and the roofs of the electric power plant buildings are reflected. The historical buildings of the surroundings, damaged over time, and the brick decorations, hidden under the layers of plasterwork, have been restored.[26] The construction of the building is based on reinforced concrete cores and on a steel support, between which, as if it had been a bridge, a steel truss stretches. The historical buildings house the archives, a multi-functional room, as well as administration and research rooms.[27]

The building received the SARP Award in 2014, as well as the architectural award of the monthly *Polityka* in the same year.

PORTA POSNANIA (ICHOT) IN POZNAN, 2013

ARCHITECTURE:	Ad Artis Architects: Arkadiusz Emerla, Maciej Wojda, Piotr Jagiełłowicz, Wojtek Kasinowicz
Investor:	The city of Poznan
Floor Space:	5,070 m²
Investment Cost:	100 M PLN
Design:	2009–2010
Completion:	2013

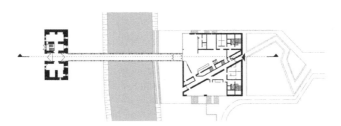

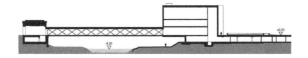

Figure 3.13 Porta Posnania (ICHOT), floor plan and section.
Source: Filip Zamiatnin/book authors.

Porta Posnania Interactive Center of Cathedral Island (Interaktywne Centrum Historii Ostrowa Tumskiego – ICHOT), designed by Ad Artis Architects, is made in an image of an architectural "boat." The idea was to create a "gate of modernity." The building is an element of a road from the city center to the historical cathedral.

The building has a complex relationship with its surroundings; its function is to shorten the road from the center, as well as to educate the visitors. However, it is an independent structure whose form strongly influences the suburban landscape. Even though it is significantly smaller than the church, from the side of the city it constitutes an equally important element of the urban arrangements.

Inside, the visitor moves on a spiral road that intersects the cracks at various levels. As a result, the onlooker experiences differing views of the cathedral. The path ends on the main level of the museum, from which the visitor can cross a glass bridge over the river and find himself on Cathedral Island.

The building was distinguished in the competition Polish Cement in Architecture, while also receiving the Jan Baptysta Quadro Award for the best building in Poznan in 2014.[28]

THE WORLD WAR II MUSEUM IN GDANSK, 2016

ARCHITECTURE: Kwadrat Design Studio: Jacek Droszcz, Bazyli Domsta, Andrzej Kwieciński, Zbigniew Kowalewski
Total Area: 58,000 m²
Investment Cost: 450 M PLN
Design: 2009
Completion: 2012–2016

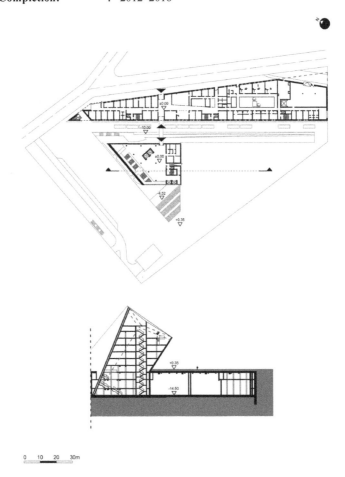

Figure 3.14 The World War II Museum in Gdańsk, floor plan and section.
Source: Marta Piórkowska/book authors.

The World War II Museum, by the Kwadrat Design Studio, is located on the Radunia Canal, on the outskirts of the Old Town in Gdansk. The land plot is situated on the premises of the Wiadrownia district, which was destroyed in 1945.

In order not to fill up the whole plot, the designers put a large part of the cubature of the building of the museum underground. This allowed them to create a square around the building, and also to show the symbolic significance of the structure, in which the subterranean space is to remind visitors of the difficult, traumatic history of the city. Apart from exhibition spaces and warehouses, the facility also boasts a cinema and conference halls. The underground segment includes a low office building. Inside the tower, there are a library, offices, lecture halls, and a restaurant with a view of the panorama of the city. The tower, which is 40.5 m high, is tilted at a 67° angle. Three of its walls are laid out with red concrete panels; the fourth, similarly to the roof, is a glazed façade.[29]

The visitors are to take part in an emotional journey, during which the concept of the building may be freely interpreted. Zbigniew Kowalewski says:

> When it comes to the tower, there is a multitude of interpretations of form. According to the interpretations of the visitors, it was to be a bomb driven into the ground, a submarine that is about to surface, a tenement house captured at the moment of its downfall, the Eye of Providence watching over the city, and many others. In our conceptual assumptions, it was initially to simply be a dynamic form tearing apart space, screaming with its otherness, color, and arousing anxiety in the minds of the visitors.[30]

The structure received the Special Award of the President of Gdansk for the best building of 2016–2017 and was nominated for the Mies van der Rohe Award in 2019.

CULTURAL FACILITIES

126 *Presentation of Polish Examples*

THE CHOPIN CENTER IN WARSAW, 2010

ARCHITECTURE:	Bolesław Stelmach, Stelmach & Partners Architectural Office
Surface Area:	2,800 m²
Investment Cost:	36 M PLN
Design:	2005–2007
Completion:	2007–2010

Figure 3.15 The Chopin Center in Warsaw, Bolesław Stelmach, Stelmach & Partners Architectural Office, 2010.

Source: Marcin Czechowicz/Stelmach & Partners Architectural Office.

The building of the Chopin Center in Warsaw, designed by Bolesław Stelmach, is situated in the neighborhood of the Ostrogski Castle. In the assumptions of the designer, the structure was to become an image of symbolic references to the life and work of Fryderyk Chopin. The outcome of such a simple assumption was the development of an exceptionally beautiful building that stretches high above but does not overshadow the Ostrogski Castle. The building contains archives, a reading room, a bookshop, a restaurant, a café, and a small conference and concert hall. The upper stories house the offices of the Fryderyk Chopin National Institute. The technical rooms are located underground.

In response to the competition requirement, the new structure commemorates the low nineteenth-century tenement house that had been destroyed. The restored elevations out of prefabricated concrete slabs create the plinth, out of which a glass-and-steel construction of the Chopin Center emerges. From the side of the Ostrogski Castle, the elevation of the Center is completely glazed. The elevations from the side of Tamka and Ordynacka Streets are made out of steel and glass with sanded screens.

The construction of the building is made out of reinforced concrete and steel. The subterranean levels are designed in diaphragm walls out of hydraulic concrete.[31] The concept of the building assumed finishing in architectural concrete. Due to the contractor's faults, the visible errors had to be repaired. This was done by processing and concrete texturing through cutting, graining, and chipping off. The manual craftwork provided the architecture with a new esthetic value that is seldom seen in concrete constructions.[32]

In 2010, the building of the Chopin Center was nominated for the Mies van der Rohe Award, while in the same year, Bolesław Stelmach received the SARP Honorary Award.

THE SŁUŻEWSKI HOUSE OF CULTURE IN WARSAW, 2013

ARCHITECTURE:	WWAA, Marcin Mostafa and Natalia Paszkowska; 137kilo Architekci, Architect Jan Sukiennik
Surface Area:	2,969 m²
Investment Cost:	16 M PLN
Design:	2008
Completion:	2013

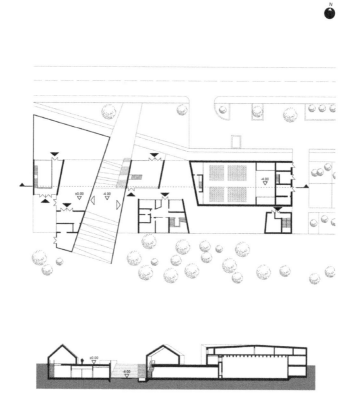

Figure 3.16 The Służewski House of Culture in Warsaw, WWAA, 137kilo, floor plan and section.

Source: Marta Piórkowska/book authors.

The Służewski House of Culture in Warsaw, by WWAA and 137kilo, is a reflection of the dreams about the cozy, rural past.

The whole is reminiscent of a village with several wooden houses, a bridge, a place to cultivate plants, and an enclosure for pets. The complex of rather-small buildings with a gable roof is situated near large-size apartment buildings and seems to be a way to transport the rural traditions and a dream of countryside breakfast and insert them into a contemporary space of a metropolitan apartment complex.

The central part of the complex and the main entrance are found in a gorge below the level of the ground. The entrance zone functions as a stage during open-air spectacles. Such a form of the building allows the interior to be linked to its surroundings. The functional program was planned in such a way, so as to create additional buildings that can function jointly or independently of one another.

The area around the buildings becomes a public space that allows for an extension of its impact outside the boundaries of the buildings.[33]

The design received the 1st Architectural Prize of the Polish monthly *Polityka*.

THE SHAKESPEARE THEATRE IN GDANSK, 2014

ARCHITECTURE: The ATI Design Group (Temporary Entrepreneurial Association), Architect Renato Rizzi – PRO.TEC.O. S.C.R.L
Surface Area: 12,241 m^2
Investment Cost: 93.8 M PLN
Design: 2008–2014
Completion: 2011–2014

Figure 3.17 The Shakespeare Theatre in Gdańsk, the ATI Design Group, Renato Rizzi, 2014.

Source: Matteo Piazza.

The Shakespeare Theatre, designed by Renato Rizzi and the ATI Design Group, is situated on the border of the Główne Miasto and Stare Przedmieście districts. The building was created in 2014 according to the design of Renato Rizzi and is an effect of a competition that took place in 2005.[34]

The external walls, referred to by the architect as "external edges," are public transport routes that surround the building. These are also escape routes from the theater area. People who move about on these routes find themselves 6 m above the entrance level, and from there they can admire the panorama of the city. The courtyards, the administration building, as well as the heart and soul of this place – the theater – are all visible from this vantage point. Due to the requirements of the functioning of stage fixtures, above the theater itself there is an 18 m high tower. All these parts are made out of brick, referencing the Gothic architecture of the city. The classical brick color scheme was broken up with the black color of the building material, which distinguishes the building.

The ribbing of the walls, which is reminiscent of Gothic abutments, reflects the rhythm of a module construction and transfers the load from the roof of the building. The retractable, two-winged roof allows for the organization of spectacles under the open sky and provides additional possibilities for stagings.

The interior is predominantly bright in its color scheme and boasts wooden finishing. The theater stage is movable, which allows for the audience to be placed in front of it or around in 51 modules. The technical equipment of the stage is found below its level and above in the aforementioned tower. The administration is located in a separate two-story building. It houses offices, a restaurant, and the wardrobe department. The roof has a terrace that is accessible via outside paths.[35]

The building was a finalist in the Life in Architecture competition in 2015, was the recipient of the Architizer A+ Award 2016, and was nominated for the Mies van der Rohe Award in 2015.

HOUSES
OF MUSIC

134 Presentation of Polish Examples

THE KRZYSZTOF PENDERECKI EUROPEAN CENTER FOR MUSIC IN LUSŁAWICE, 2013

ARCHITECTURE:	DDJM Design Studio – Marek Dunikowski, Jarosław Kutniowski, Wojciech Miecznikowski
Surface Area:	14,123 m^2
Investment Cost:	65 M PLN
Design:	2003–2013
Completion:	2012–2013

Figure 3.18 The Krzysztof Penderecki European Center for Music in Lusławice, DDJM, 2013.

Source: Marcin Czechowicz.

The Krzysztof Penderecki European Center for Music, designed by DDJM Design Studio, is found in the small village of Lusławice. The patron and the man behind the Center was Krzysztof Penderecki (1932–2020), who wanted to create a place that would aid young talented musicians.

The rather-simple body of the building is an elongated cuboid that is surrounded by a wooden portico and is the principal and the highest element of the interior, which houses the concert hall. The simplicity of the form, but also the material from which it is made, causes the Center to be the dominant form in the idyllic landscape of the village.

The most important place and the only large building is the concert hall for 650 people. It is an independent construction. The interior is finished with wood, and on the walls the vertical rhythm of the abutments is clearly visible. The panels in the coffered ceiling have a varied angle of incline, which provides good acoustics for the interior. The stage, thanks to its large size and the possibility to change its geometry, allows for concerts of numerous types of chamber, symphonic, and choir music. The concert hall is surrounded by a foyer, from which the didactic part of the building can be accessed through the atrium. It is here where the chamber concert hall is located, along with the conference halls, a recording studio, and a library. The functional system is supplemented by a residential area for 100 people.

The building was nominated for the Mies van der Rohe Award in 2015 and received the Annual SARP Award in 2012.[36]

THE "SYMFONIA" CENTER OF MUSICAL SCIENCE AND EDUCATION IN KATOWICE, 2007

ARCHITECTURE:	Tomasz Konior, Krzysztof Barysz, Konior Studio
Surface Area:	7,330 m^2; along with the old building, 14,119 m^2
Investment Cost:	55 M PLN
Design:	2003–2006
Completion:	2005–2007

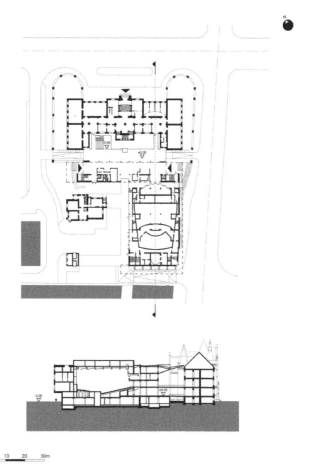

Figure 3.19 The "Symfonia" Center of Musical Science and Education, Tomasz Konior, Krzysztof Barysz, Konior Studio, 2007, floor plan and section.

Source: Marta Piórkowska/book authors.

The building of the "Symfonia," designed by K. Barysz and T. Konior, is part of the Academy of Music in Katowice and is situated near an old cemetery and nineteenth-century residential and office buildings. The competition and the subsequent expansion of the Karol Szymanowski Academy of Music was one of the first significant architectural investments in the city after the year 2000. In 2007, Tomasz Masłowski, an architecture critic, at that time wrote that the building "seems to be a turning point in the architecture of Katowice. Because finally after years of meaninglessness here is a building which is an event."[37]

The new structure emerges immediately next to the old building of the Academy from 1898. The large rectangular body with a small number of windows is separated from the old richly decorated building by a glazed atrium. Both the buildings are made of brick; however, their form and decoration distinctly show two different eras. The new form brings forth positive connotations with local modernism from the interwar period. It is adorned with the delicate protruding of the bricks from the wall face and an emphasis on the shape of the windows, which sound off with long cracks in the façade of the elevation bricks removed from the surface.

The atrium is a public space with a café, a shop, and a small amphitheater. It is also a meeting and resting place for students and inhabitants of the area. The richly decorated Neo-Gothic façade of the old building creates the atmosphere of the interior at the meeting point of the old and new architecture. From the atrium, we can enter the old building, while access to various levels is granted by concrete platforms. From this new space, we come into the elegant, new concert hall for 480 listeners. This is the first concert hall in Poland that utilizes reverberation chambers that allow for a "changing" of the hall cubature and influence its acoustic properties.

The quality with which the designers paid respects to the historical building of the Academy, adding a new value to it, has received praise and admiration. Among the numerous awards, there are the Grand Prix of the Architecture of the Year of the Silesian Voivodeship in 2008, the Annual SARP Award in 2007 for the best completion of a structure, the Friendly and Inclusive Space Award at the XXIII UIA Congress in Torino, and a nomination for the Mies van der Rohe Award.[38]

THE PODLASKA OPERA IN BIALYSTOK, 2012

ARCHITECTURE:	Marek Budzyński Architect – Marek Budzyński, Krystyna Ilmurzyńska, Zbigniew Badowski
Surface Area:	16,109 m²
Investment Cost:	181.9 M PLN
Design:	2005–2007
Completion:	2012

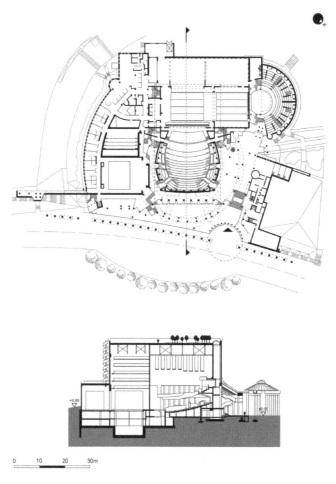

Figure 3.20 The Podlaska Opera in Białystock, Marek Budzyński, 2012, floor plan and section.

Source: Filip Zamiatnin/book authors.

The Podlaska Opera in Białystok, designed by Marek Budzyński, was created on the site of the existing but neglected Czesław Niemen Amphitheatre. Prior to World War II, Białystok had a large Jewish population. The multitude of cultures and diversity of traditions that were present in the area convinced the architects to be inspired by places of worship and "holy" hills from different cultures.[39]

The bright, simple body of the concert hall emerges from the large overgrown roof. In the architecture of the building, modern elements associated with high-tech architecture were combined with symbols of the past. The glazed foyer hidden behind a "Greek" colonnade is an extension of the public space of the adjacent park. The amphitheater is connected with the Opera body.

The concert hall can fit nearly 1,000 listeners; the audience is horseshoe-shaped, and the balcony is based on the geometry of a right angle. In describing the interior, Marek Budzyński sys that "the interior of the hall was created as a combination of opposites – a traditional opera and contemporary flexibility."[40] In the assumptions of the architects, the character of the interior references secessionism and art deco; it is believed to be the "last contact point creating interiors which as a rule are user-friendly, taking full advantage of the integration of architecture, sculpture, painting, and craft."[41] Realistic sculptures of musicians, singers, and dancers completed by Dominik Wdowski project out of the dark-blue concrete walls.

The building received the AEDIFICIUM ANNO 2009–2012 Grand Prix of the Białystok branch of SARP.

THE MIECZYSŁAW KARŁOWICZ PHILHARMONIC IN SZCZECIN, 2014

ARCHITECTURE:	Estudio Barozzi Veiga
Surface Area:	12,734 m²
Investment Cost:	118,9 M PLN
Design:	2007–2009
Completion:	2014

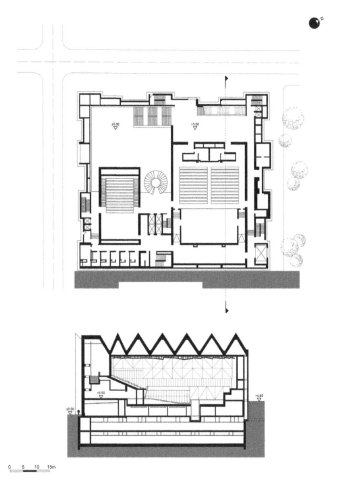

Figure 3.21 The Mieczysław Karłowicz Philharmonic in Szczecin, Estudio Barozzi Viega, 2014, floor plan and section.

Source: Marta Piórkowska/book authors.

The Mieczysław Karłowicz Philharmonic building in Szczecin, 2014, was erected based on the design of the architects Fabrizio Barozzi and Alberto Veiga from Barcelona, who won a competition in 2007. Architecturally, the building draws inspiration from numerous ideas while also introducing various esthetics, combining them in a surprising work. As a result, the structure has become a "symbol" of the city quarter, reduced to a system of boxes and pyramids, bereft of architectural elements: stories, doors, windows, and details. The visually uniform elevation consists of vertical slats made of lacquered-in-white profiled sheet metal that are situated against the background of frosted glass. Over 25,000 LEDs were also mounted, which, controlled by a computer system, illuminate the building with various colors.[42]

The building elevation is multi-layered. Great emphasis was placed on its proper acoustic and thermal insulation. In the external walls of the building, there are ventilation installations of the heating and electrical power systems of the building.[43]

Modern material and synthetic form make this facility distinguishable from its surroundings, showing the difference in its image in daylight and nightlight. This ability to "bring together" contradictions is also visible inside the building, which is a non-uniform tale about "stories" on a small and large scale, drawing ideas from different places and various periods in history. An example of this is the contrast between the large foyer, which is a direct reference to modernist ideas, and the main concert hall for nearly 1,000 persons, which recalls the golden richness of the Baroque.[44]

The Spanish architects from the Estudio Barozzi Veiga, in designing the Szczecin Philharmonic, made attempts to entrench the building into the spatial and cultural context of the city. They assumed that the form of the building would, on one hand, be contextual; on the other, it would become "a physical structure filled with life, movement, sounds."[45] It must be mentioned that the scale of the audience, with fewer than 1,000 seats, seriously inhibits the possibilities to play music, especially large-scale symphonic pieces.

The Mieczysław Karłowicz Philharmonic is the first building in Poland which won the Mies van der Rohe Award in 2015.

THE JORDANKI CULTURAL AND CONGRESS CENTER IN TORUN, 2015

ARCHITECTURE:	Fernando Menis
Surface Area:	22,000 m^2
Investment Cost:	225 M PLN
Design:	2008
Completion:	2015

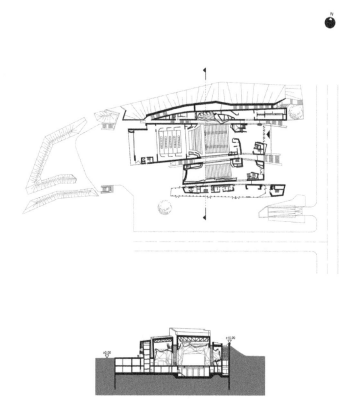

Figure 3.22 The Jordanki Cultural and Congress Center in Toruń, Fernando Menis, floor plan and section.

Source: Filip Zamiatnin/book authors.

The CKK Jordanki building, designed by Fernando Menis, is located in the direct neighborhood of the Torun Old Town, which is part of the UNESCO World Heritage list[46] and has, for the last several years, attracted 1.5 million tourists annually.[47]

During the works on the CKK Jordanki, the functional program of the building was extended in order for the concert hall to become a multifunctional facility. The form of the building is a sculpted body, which brings to mind the image of a rock or stone. In the assumptions of the architects, the form was not to disturb the green ring that surrounds the Old Town. As Fernando Menis recalls, "the activities which we had proposed in our competition work are elements immersed in the green zone, constituting islands in its interior."[48] The body of the building is made up of a mixture of concrete and bricks or Picado stones.[49] The scale of the structure matches the protected, historical buildings, leaving room around for public spaces.

The interior of the building is complex in its form. Thanks to movable elements of the walls and ceiling, the concert hall can change its dimensions and acoustic properties to accommodate music of all kind – symphonic, chamber, classical, opera, pop, or rock – but also congresses and spectacles.[50]

The acoustic properties and the inclusion of the body into the context were the reasons for the building receiving the SARP Award in 2015 in the category of public utility structure – cultural facility.

SPORTS
FACILITIES

146 *Presentation of Polish Examples*

FLYSPOT IN MORY, NEAR WARSAW, 2014

ARCHITECTURE:	The Lewicki Łatak Design Studio; Architects: Kazimierz Łatak, Piotr Lewicki
Total Area:	926 m²
Investment Cost:	24 M PLN
Design:	2012–2014
Completion:	2013–2014

Figure 3.23 Flyspot in Mory, Lewicki Łatak Design Studio, 2014.
Source: Wojciech Kryński/Lewicki Łatak Design Studio.

The Flyspot building, designed by Piotr Lewicki and Kazimierz Łatak, was created in the years 2013–2104 in Mory, near Warsaw.

The architects wanted the building to distinguish itself from its chaotic urban context near the highway. As a result, the form was designed in such a way as to underline the overcoming of gravity by the power of the wind. It is a reinforced concrete construction with walls and ceilings of different thicknesses. The structure's dimensions are 33 m × 22 at the base, a height of 38 m, out of which 11 m is above the ground.

The main part of the structure is a vertical aerodynamic tunnel in which a person can float thanks to the speed of the air (300 km/h). The structure of the building is centered on the tunnel with a square cross section whose side is 7.5 m long. Inside is the basic technology of an aerodynamic tunnel, with a closed circuit. There are rooms placed around the tunnel in a spiral manner, including the reception desk, offices, hotel rooms, and conference halls.[51] The part in which people float is glazed and is reminiscent of a glass cylinder.

EDUCATIONAL FACILITIES

THE COPERNICUS SCIENCE CENTER IN WARSAW, 2011

ARCHITECTURE:	Laboratorium Architektury RAr2 Jan Kubec
Surface Area:	19,150 m²
Investment Cost:	360 M PLN
Design:	2005–2007
Completion:	2008–2011

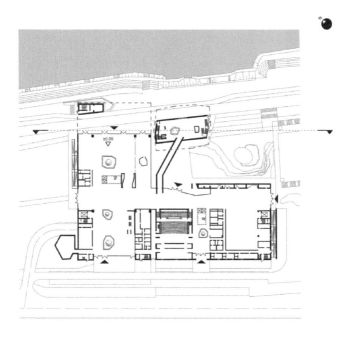

Figure 3.24 Copernicus Science Center in Warsaw, Jan Kubec, 2011, floor plan and section.

Source: Marta Piórkowska/book authors.

The Copernicus Science Center in Warsaw, designed by Jan Kubec, 2011, is found on the banks of the Vistula River. The idea behind the design was to continue the landscape of the Vistula River banks. Jan Kubec says:

> From the very beginning we were shaping something that was not standard architecture, but a natural enclave, which can be treated less strictly, which is to be free, just as the wild banks of the Vistula. The greatest challenge was putting such enormous cubature, 20 thousand square meters, on a rather small 4.5-hectare land plot, where we also had to fit the Discovery Park. . . . We decided to turn all of the arrangements into a public space . . . if we would like to consider the Copernicus Science Center, this cannot be done outside the context of its surroundings. We can go through the building, under it, and also above it and this was the key issue during the design process.[52]

Here we have an open amphitheater, a planetarium in the shape of a rock, and the Discovery Park, which is connected to the main exhibition space by a promenade. All these functions are connected by an agora that is dedicated to the organization of temporary exhibitions.

The main building of the CSC is two-story, 12 m high, L-shaped, and covered by a green roof. It contains a rich functional program that consists of the exhibition space, an auditorium, workshops, and offices, as well as a café, the necessary infrastructure, and conference halls. The roof houses an observation deck and a geological garden open for visitors. The idea was to transport the riverbank terrain that was now occupied by the Center onto the upper story of the building.

The Center, which received an award in the "Life in Architecture" competition, was also nominated for the Mies van der Rohe Award in 2011.

THE FINANCE FACULTY OF THE UNIVERSITY OF ECONOMICS IN CRACOW, 2004

ARCHITECTURE: Atelier Loegler
Surface Area: No data available
Investment Cost: 40 M PLN
Design: 1999–2001
Completion: 2000–2004

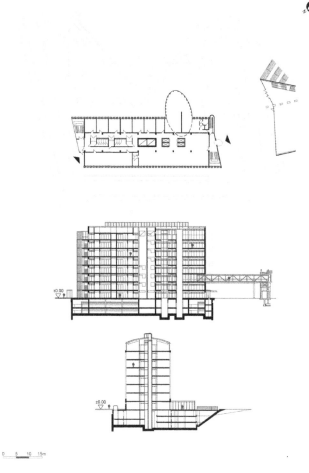

Figure 3.25 The Finance Faculty of the University of Economics in Cracow, Atelier Loegler, 2004, floor plan and section.

Source: Paulina Nagel/book authors.

The building of the Faculty of Finance and Law of the University of Economics, designed by Romuald Loegler, is found in the center of Cracow. The principal axis of the university campus is marked by Neo-Renaissance buildings designed in 1893 by Tadeusz Stryjeński and Władysław Ekielski, as well as two buildings completed by the Romuald Loegler design studio. The first, a didactic and sports facility, was created in the 1990s; the second, the Faculty of Finance, in 2004.

The building of the Faculty of Finance and Law is distinguished by its façade, which is made up of a rhythm of vertical narrow lesenes finished off with brick. The tightly spaced lesenes harmoniously shape the beauty of the long high wall, but they also fulfill a constructional role. Using steel elements to connect with ceilings of subsequent floors, they enable thermal insulation to be used on the outer side of the supports. Visually, the lesenes appear to be a brick openwork placed on top of the glass façade. The body is distinguished by its glazed top story, as well as the side walls with diagonally placed staircases. The facility includes rooms for academic staff and students, didactic rooms and lecture halls, as well as offices.[53] Its creator, Romuald Loegler, received the Honorary SARP Award for this design in 1994.

THE BIAŁOŁEKA MIDDLE SCHOOL AND CULTURAL CENTER IN WARSAW, 2005

ARCHITECTURE:	Tomasz Konior, Konior Studio, Tomasz Danielec
Surface Area:	7,713 m²
Investment Cost:	No data available
Design:	2000–2002
Completion:	2004–2005

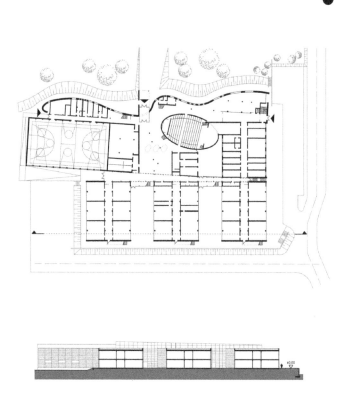

Figure 3.26 The Białołeka Middle School and Cultural Center in Białołęka, Konior Studio, 2005, floor plan and section.

Source: Filip Zamiatnin/book authors.

The building of the Middle School in Białołęka, designed by Tomasz Konior, is the designer's personal response to the context of the landscape along the Vistula River.

The complex consists of a cultural center, with a large auditorium for nearly 400 spectators, a public library, a sports center, and a school for 800 students.

Behind the brick wall, there is a glazed entrance hall, which ensures independent access to all the principal functions, allowing for independence of functioning. The distinguishing factor in the form is the oval auditorium, which seems to be an autonomous element of the structure of the complex, a form that is clearly visible in the figure of the building.

The second, educational part of the school is located in three segments placed parallel to one another. They are glazed in order to preserve a view of the patios. The end walls, made of large concrete prefabricates, have only a few windows. The dominant elements in the finishing, on the elevation, and inside the building are concrete, glass, and brick.

The 70 m long undulating wall is the building's calling card, connecting the structure throughout. The curved line is a reference to the nearby riverbank of the Vistula. It emphasizes the expressive character of architecture, especially in comparison with the remaining part of the arrangements, which is pragmatically based on right-angle geometry, which allows for creating interiors of various shapes. It also facilitates the creation of viewing corridors, which take advantage of the lush greenery.[54]

The structure received the following awards: the main award Polish Concrete in Architecture, 2006; among the top 20 buildings completed after 1989, Icon of Architecture 2005; the Leonardo Award in the International Biennale of Young Architects in Minsk in the category public utility building in 2007.

THE FACULTY OF NEOPHILOLOGY AND APPLIED LINGUISTICS OF THE UNIVERSITY OF WARSAW, 2012

ARCHITECTURE:	APA Kuryłowicz & Associates
Surface Area:	42,772 m²
Investment Cost:	66.3 M PLN
Design:	2006
Completion:	2012

Figure 3.27 The Faculty of Neophilology and Applied Linguistics of the University of Warsaw, APA Kuryłowicz & Associates.

Source: Tomasz Kubaczyk.

The building of the Philology Faculties of the University of Warsaw, by APA Kuryłowicz & Associates, is found near the University of Warsaw Library. The winners of the competition were announced in 2006, but for financial reasons, the deadline for its completion was extended.

The main façade of the building of the Faculty of Neophilology, which is opposite the library, is fully glazed and reflects the elevation of its neighbor. This close proximity makes the references to the architecture of the library building natural. At the basis of such a concept was the willingness to create a structure in which the characters of the interior and the exterior are connected with each other and which "undergoes constant changes, where the space is alive and organic."[55]

The main entrance hall, which is several stories high, is found in the corner of the building. The ground floor houses food services, while the roof boasts a green terrace. The elevations have various shapes. One is fully glazed, with green accents, which are a reference to a structure of a hedge. The other is solid, finished with panels made of patinated copper and yellow HPL panels. The rooms are centered on the courtyard. The interiors were designed in such a way as to allow the people moving around inside the building to always maintain eye contact with the outside. They were designed in distinct colors, which are assigned to various functions. The completed building is an element of larger arrangements in which there are five courtyards placed parallel to the axis of the building.[56]

The design received an award in a competition titled Warsaw-Friendly Building in 2012.

THE KRZYSZTOF KIEŚLOWSKI FILM SCHOOL IN KATOWICE, 2017

ARCHITECTURE:	BAAS, Grupa 5 Architects, Małeccy Design Studio
Surface Area:	7,035 m²
Investment Cost:	38.5 M PLN
Design:	2011–2014
Completion:	2014–2017

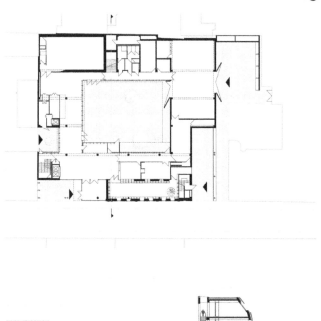

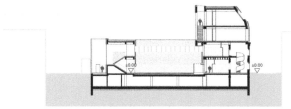

Figure 3.28 The Krzysztof Kieślowski Film School in Katowice, BAAS, Grupa 5 Architects, Małeccy Design Studio, 2017, floor plan and section.

Source: Paulina Nagel/book authors.

The building of the Silesian film school, designed by BAAS from Spain, the Grupa 5 Architekci from Warsaw, and the Małeccy Design Studio from Katowice, was created in Katowice near the University of Silesia. The complex of the Krzysztof Kieślowski Film School buildings supplements the frontage of a street and neighbors the university buildings.

The competition organized in Katowice in 2001 was won by a concept in which – apart from the simplicity of form – it was proposed to take advantage of the structure of the old historical building. The reflection of such a concept is the building elevation – besides historical brick walls, it is made out of ceramic blocks. The material, which is similar to bricks, which characterize surrounding buildings, is affectionately referred to by the students as "TV sets," and it continues the tradition of brick buildings, creating an interesting and, at the same time, simple architecture. The view from the interior and the terrace located on the roof is of neglected, old brick outbuildings.

Apart from the didactic and office rooms, the building also houses a recording studio, a cinema hall, production rooms, as well as places designated for rest and integration. The faculty library is located in the historical structure of the building.

The design was included on the shortlist to receive the Mies van der Rohe Award in 2019 and won numerous distinctions, such as the Grand Prix of the Annual SARP Award and the Body of the Year Award.

LIBRARIES

162 *Presentation of Polish Examples*

THE CENTER OF ACADEMIC INFORMATION AND THE ACADEMIC LIBRARY IN KATOWICE, 2011

ARCHITECTURE:	HS99, Architects Dariusz Herman, Wojciech Subalski, Piotr Śmierzewski
Surface Area:	13,260 m²
Investment Cost:	57.5 M PLN
Design:	2002–2004
Completion:	2009–2011

Figure 3.29 The Center of Academic Information and the Academic Library in Katowice, HS99, 2011.
Source: Dominika Werczyńska.

The Center of Academic Information and the Academic Library, designed by HS99, were created at the center of the academic campus of the University of Silesia, near the Katowice Culture Zone.

In 2002, the architects from the HS99 design studio won a competition for the new library of the University of Silesia. Later, it was decided that the building would also serve as the library for the University of Economics.[57] The Academic Library created in the years 2009–2011 contributed to the development of the campus.

The location, as well as the rectangular body of the building, strengthens the axial organization of the campus, which until then had been barely articulated. The simple form reflects the pragmatically and usefully solved function. The basis of the building, which is three stories high, is devoted to readers; the higher, six-story one houses a book warehouse and offices.

The elevations were laid out with red sandstone which is known as Kahan red. The sandstone is a material often used in architecture, but this design attempts to give it a new expression. The panels used in the elevations are smaller in the upper parts of the building, while in the cracks between them, there are 4,004 windows. Both the great number of windows as well as the non-uniform dimensions of the sandstone panels conceal the scale of the library. The number of stories is difficult to make out. Here is what the architects have to say about it: "A lack of noticeable scale causes the monolith seen from afar to be gradually tamed. The details such as the proportions of elevations panels, irregular cutting of the sandstone panels, as well as the windows carefully nestled inside, become visible."[58]

THE RACZYŃSKI LIBRARY IN POZNAN, 2013

ARCHITECTURE:	JEMS Architekci
Total Area:	14,881 m²
Investment Cost:	72.8 M PLN
Design:	2009
Completion:	2013

Figure 3.30 The Raczyński Library in Poznań, JEMS Architects, 2014.
Source: Juliusz Sokołowski/JEMS Architekci.

The Raczyński Library, designed by JEMS Architekci, is situated in downtown Poznan and is one of the oldest libraries in Poland. It was established in 1829 by Count Edward Raczyński, and its front elevation is patterned on the eastern elevation of the Louvre.

In 2002, a decision was made to expand the library. The subsequent architectural competition was won by the Warsaw-based design studio JEMS Architekci.[59]

A new body was made, whose elevation is articulated by high concrete pillars. Their height is connected with the height of the elements of the historical elevation, which consists of a high "plinth" as well as a representative floor – the *piano nobile*. A distinct horizontal division, visible on the historical façade, was interpreted by the creators of the new building in an interesting way. The dense vertical division of concrete columns gives off the impression of a uniform "heavy" wall, and upon closer inspection, the elevation becomes more transparent. The delicate articulation of horizontal divisions becomes obvious, relating to the historical building. The glazing, removed from the external face of the wall, beneficially disperses the sunlight in the interior.

The previous small entrance to the library was kept – the old building is accessed through a glazed walkway. Similar to the historical building, the reading room and the catalog are found on the level of the *piano nobile*. Below is a single-space library, while the lowest story houses an art gallery, a café, and a children's library.

The spacious interiors do not have columns. The four great cores in the corners support the upper stories of the warehouses.[60]

CHURCHES

THE CHURCH OF THE ASCENSION OF THE LORD IN WARSAW, 1990

ARCHITECTURE:	Marek Budzyński, Zbigniew Badowski
Surface Area:	7,411 m^2
Investment Cost:	No data available
Design:	1980–1985
Completion:	1982–1990

Figure 3.31 The Church of the Ascension of the Lord in Warsaw, Marek Budzyński, Zbigniew Badowski, 1990.

Source: Adrian Grycuk, own work, CC BY-SA 3.0 pl, https://commons.wikimedia.org/w/index.php?curid=103477964.

The Church of the Ascension of the Lord, by Marek Budzyński and Zbigniew Badowski, was erected on the site of a former marketplace that was demolished in 1979. The body of the church distinguishes itself from the blocks made out of large panels with its form and materiality. The main elevation from the side of the town square is a form reminiscent of arrangements of the Baroque.[61] It is made of brick, and the stone plinth can bring to mind rural church architecture. The entrance is accentuated by a large window in the shape of a cross as well as the entrance openings topped off with arches.

The spacious interior relates to a basilica, while the weak additional lighting of the large space creates an atmosphere that contributes to contemplation. The reinforced concrete arches of the side naves are not placed on top of columns that would separate the main nave from the side one – they rather seem to be floating in the air.

The details of the building, as well as its finishing, contribute to the form boasting a complex religious symbolism. However, its message was difficult to accept by the faithful, which is further testified to by the words of the art historian Rev. Andrzej Luft, PhD:

> The body of this church is certainly an architectural jewel surrounded by blocks-boxes. However, the inhumane interior arouses many objections. The stone, unsupported arches give off the impression as if they were to fall at any moment, that is why mass-goers avoid these places. Further anxiety is also introduced by the image of the crucifix which is inconsistent with Christian iconography. The façade and the wall of the presbytery look as if the cross had been torn out of them.[62]

VOTUM ALEKSA IN TARNOW UPON THE VISTULA, 2011

ARCHITECTURE:	Beton, Marta Rowińska, and Lech Rowiński
Surface Area:	68 m²
Investment Cost:	80,000 PLN
Design:	2007
Completion:	2007–2011

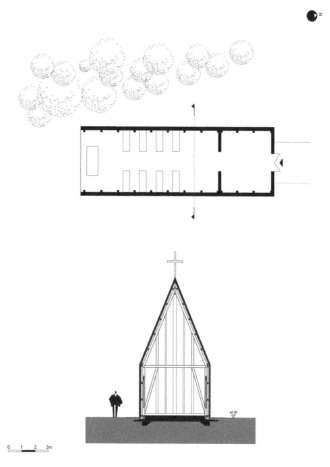

Figure 3.32 Votum Aleksa in Tarnów, Beton, 2011.
Source: Jakub Certowicz.

The Votum Aleksa Chapel, designed by Marta and Lech Rowiński, distinguishes itself with a specific modesty of form, material, and the technology employed. The architects were entrusted with the task to design a church, which, similarly to a former one, would be wooden and whose technology would allow the building to be completed by local craftspeople. The location of the church restored past glory to the neglected bank of the Vistula.[63]

The chapel is finished off with shingles, while its gabled roof visually joins to the side walls into a uniform body. The chapel stands on a concrete slab, and the construction is made out of pine planks, which are supported by wooden panels. The esthetic form of the interior results in the wooden structure becoming the principal and only decoration of the interior, in which the wall opposite the entrance is fully glazed, providing a view of the distant horizon and the river. While the front wall is covered with full-sized wooden panels, the black horizontal rods mark the entrance, serving as hinges for the wooden door.

The references to the rural identity of the place as well as the social aspects of the design resulted in the building being the first structure in Poland that found itself on the shortlist for the Mies van der Rohe Award in 2011.[64] The building is the "youngest historic monument" in Poland. In December 2022, 11 years after its construction, it was entered in the register of historic landmarks.[65]

172 Presentation of Polish Examples

Notes

1 W. Leśnikowski, *"Focusa" pokusa monumentalna,* www.budynekfocus.com/pl# [access: 23.09.2019].
2 Kuryłowicz & Associates, *Focus,* www.apaka.com.pl/pl/projekty/budynek-biurowy-fokus [access: 3.10.19].
3 W. Leśnikowski, *"Focusa" pokusa monumentalna.*
4 cf. G. Stiasny, *Od A Do Z – Alfabet Architektury,* "Architektura-Murator" 2004, no. 10, p. 110.
5 J.S. Majewski, *Giełda,* "Architektura-Murator" 2000, vol. 9, no. 72, pp. 32–40.
6 *Budynek BRE Banku w Bydgoszczy,* Architekturamurator-plus.pl/kolekcja-architektury/budynek-bre-banku-w-bydgoszczy_3726.html [access: 4.09.2019].
7 *Architektura kontekstu. An interview with Andrzej Bulanda and Włodzimierz Mucha, the Owners of the Bulanda & Mucha Architekci Design Studio, Conducted by Teodor Wernicki,* "Sto Journal" 2007, no. 1, p. 2.
8 G. Stiasny, *Agora,* "Architektura-Murator" 2002, no. 5 (91), pp. 9–18, and J. Szczepanik-Dzikowski, *Założenia autorskie,* "Architektura-Murator" 2002, no. 5 (91), pp. 25–27.
9 See: D.L., *Zana House – Milczący Biurowiec,* www.bryla.pl/bryla/1,85301,7740 864,Zana_House___milczacy_biurowiec.html [access: 23.09.2019].
10 Ibid. and *Do środka,* "Sztuka architektury", http://sztuka-architektury.pl/article/3631/do-srodka [access: 23.09.2019].
11 *Nagroda Roku SARP wręczona!* www.sarp.org.pl/pokaz/nagroda_roku_sarp_wreczona!,1339/ [access: 02.12.2019].
12 https://lpnt.pl/ [access: 28.11.2019] and *Lublin Science and Technology Park/ Stelmach i Partnerzy Biuro Architektoniczne,* www.archdaily.com/614651/lublin-science-and-technology-park-stelmach-i-partnerzy-biuro-architektoniczne [access: 15.10.2019].
13 *O parku,* https://lpnt.pl/o-parku [access: 28.11.2019].
14 Ibid.
15 K. Mycielski, *Wieżowiec Q22 w Warszawie,* "Architektura-Murator" 2017, no. 2, pp. 56–62, and Kuryłowicz & Associates, *Q22* www.apaka.com.pl/pl/publikacje/wiezowiec-q22-w-warszawie [access: 30.10.2019].
16 www.mvrdv.nl/projects/51/baltyk?photo=5849 [access: 3.10.2018] and *Bałtyk w Poznaniu to najpiękniejszy budynek w Polsce,* www.bryla.pl/bryla/7,85301,21 901211,baltyk-w-poznaniu-to-najpiekniejszy-budynek-w-polsce-oto.html [access: 18.09.2019].
17 Ibid.; *Bałtyk Office Building,* https://miesarch.com/work/3927 [access: 18.09.2019] and *Bałtyk Tower. Innowacyjność i wizja,* builderpolska.pl/2017/10/02/bałtyk-towe-innowacyjność-i-wizja/ [access: 15.12.2019].
18 J. Łujaszewski, *Bałtyk najlepszym budynkiem roku w Poznaniu. Nagroda Quadro pierwszy raz dla cudzoziemca: 300 makiet i kilka lat prób,* poznan.wyborcza.pl/poznan/7,36001,24054188,300-makiet-i-kilka-lat-prob-nagroda-quadro-po-razpierwszy.html [access: 18.09.2019].
19 M. Budzyński, Z. Badowski, *Założenia autorskie,* "Architektura-Murator" 2000, no. 1 (64), p. 28, and A. Bojańczyk, *Siedziba Sądu Najwyższego,* www.sn.pl/osadzienajwyzszym/SitePages/Siedziba.aspx [access: 18.09. 2019].
20 M. Budzyński, Z. Badowski, *Założenia . . . ,* p. 31.
21 A. Bojańczyk, *Siedziba Sądu . . .*
22 *Sąd Najwyższy,* "Architektura-Murator" 2000, no. 1 (64), pp. 12–22.
23 *Budynek Sądu Okręgowego,* https://npp.slaskie.pl/vote/content/edition_5_project_130 [access: 19.09.2019] and *District Court in Katowice,* miesarch.com/work/1999 [access: 19.09.2019].

24 *Toruń na liście UNESCO*, www.wizja.krakow.pl/pl/projects/41 [access: 19.09.2019].
25 We have included the drawing at the end of the book.
26 *Budowa Muzeum Tadeusz Kantora i nowej siedziby CRICOTEKI*, http://cricote kawbudowie.pl/pl,dokumentacja-fotograficzna [access: 19.09.2019].
27 D. Załuski, Cricoteka, in: *Form Follows Freedom*..., pp. 200–207, and *O nas*, www.cricoteka.pl/pl/o-nas/ [access: 19.09.2019].
28 *ICHOT. Brama Poznania z nagrodą Jana Baptysty Quadro*, https://sztuka-architektury.pl/article/2953/ichot-brama-poznania-z-nagroda-jana-baptysty-quadro [access: 16.12.2019].
29 *Nominacje do nagrody im. Miesa van der Rohe 2019 – Muzeum II Wojny Światowej w Gdańsku*, http://archinea.pl/nominacje-do-nagrody-im-miesa-van-der-rohe-2019-muzeum-ii-wojny-swiatowej-w-gdansku/ [access: 16.12.2019].
30 K. Sołoducha, *Życie na trzech poziomach – an interview*, http://sztuka-architektury.pl/article/10301/muzeum-drugiej-wojny-zycia-na-trzech-poziomach [access: 3.10.2019].
31 *The Chopin Center*, https://miesarch.com/work/493 [access: 3.10.2019].
32 *Zanurzony w życiu*, sztuka-architektury.pl/article/3665/zanurzony-w-zyciu [access: 3.10.2019].
33 N. Juzwa, A. Gil, K. Ujma-Wąsowicz, *Almost Human Architecture*, http://kaiu.pan.pl/index.php?option=com_content&view=article&id=463&catid=60&Itemid=56 [access: 3.10.2019].
34 A. Cymer, *Szekspir zamieszka w Gdańsku*, http://sztuka-architektury.pl/article/4541/szekspir-zamieszka-w-gdansku [access: 24.09.2019].
35 *Gdansk Shakespearean Theatre/Renato Rizzi*, www.archdaily.com/595895/gdansk-shakespearean-theatre-renato-rozzi [access: 24.09.2019].
36 T. Malkowski, *Europejskie Centrum Muzyki Krzysztofa Pendereckiego*, in: *Form Follows Freedom*..., pp. 168–175 and *The Krzysztof Penderecki European Centre for Music*, www.miesarch.com/work/606 [access: 6.12.2019] and *O nas*, https://penderecki-center.pl/o-nas [access: 6.12.2019].
37 T. Malkowski, *Ceglana melodia*, "Architektura i Biznes" 2008, no. 6, p. 64.
38 Ibid. and *Science and Musical Education Center Symphony/Konior Studio*, www.archdaily.com/511867/science-and-musical-education-center-symphony-konior-studio/, ISSN 0719–8884 [access: 4.09.2019].
39 M. Budzyński, *Walka o osiągnięcie jedni*, "Architektura-Murator" 2012, no. 11 (218), p. 60.
40 Ibid., p. 63.
41 Ibid.
42 *Filharmonia Szczecińska. Ikona architektury i technika*, www.muratorplus.pl/inwestycje/inwestycje-publiczne/filharmonia-szczecinska-ikona-architektury-i-technika-aa-HH3i-QBw3-TDEW.html [access: 18.06.2020].
43 *Philharmonic Hall*, www.miesarch.com/work/567 [access: 18.09.2019] and The Sika System product catalogue antygraffiti: Sikagard®-781 S, Sikagard®-77 *SIKA AT WORK, Filharmonia im. Mieczysława Karłowicza w Szczecinie*.
44 T. Malkowski, Filharmonia im. Mieczysława Karłowicza, in: *Form Follows Freedom*..., pp. 50–56.
45 M. Miłobędzki, *Nastrój kreowany światłem*, "Architektura-Murator" 2014, no. 7, p. 52.
46 *Toruń na liście UNESCO*, www.torun.pl/pl/kultura/torun-na-liscie-unesco [access: 17.06.2019].
47 *Tourism in Poland. The Number of Tourists in Torun is Systematically Increasing*, www.money.pl/gospodarka/wiadomosci/artykul/turystyka;w;polsce;systematyczni e;wzrasta;liczba;turystow;w;toruniu,154,0,1523866.html [access: 14.09.2019] oraz

174 Presentation of Polish Examples

Toruń z zeszłym roku odwiedziło aż 2,35 mln turystów, http://torun.wyborcza.pl/torun/7,48723,24699545,torun-odwiedzilo-w-zeszlym-roku-az-2-mln-turystow.html [access: 14.09.2019].

48 J. Oleksiak, *An interview with Fernando Menis*, "Archiektura i Biznes" 2009, no. 10, p. 80.

49 The first time Menis used this material was in the Magma Art and Congress (Tenerife, Canary Islands, 2005), mixing concrete with the local volcanic stone. For the CKK Jordanki, this technique was further developed and certified by the Polish Building Research Institute. cf. http://menis.es/en/portfolio/centro-de-cultura-y-congresos-ckk-jordanki/ [access: 14.09.2019].

50 *Historia budowy Centrum*, http://jordanki.torun.pl/budowa/ [access: 13.12.2019]; http://menis.es/en/portfolio/centro-de-cultura-y-congresos-ckk-jordanki/ [access: 14.09.2019] and *Jordanki Culture and Congres Centre, CKK "Jordanki"*, https://miesarch.com/work/3658 [access: 14.09.2019] and *Nagroda Roku – wyniki*, www.sarp.org.pl/pokaz/nagroda_roku-wyniki,2249/ [access: 14.09.2019].

51 *Flyspot Warsaw/Biuro Projektow Lewicki Łatak*, www.archdaily.com/903172/flyspot-warsaw-biuro-projektow-lewicki-latak [access: 3.10.2019].

52 *Jan Kubec in an interview with Tomasz Masłowski*, https://archirama.muratorplus.pl/architektura/jan-kubec-architekt-centrum-nauki-kopernik-opowiada-o-swojej-nowatorskiej-architekturze,67_1317.html?&page=1 [access: 13.09.2019].

53 G. Stiasny, *Wydział Finansów w Krakowie*, "Architektura-Murator" 2004, 12 (123), pp. 46–50, and R. Loegler, *Założenia projektowe*, "Architektura-Murator" 2004, 12 (123), p. 51.

54 In the description we used: G. Stiasny, *Szkoła w Białołęce*, "Architektura-Murator" 2005, no 10 (133), pp. 42–44 and T. Konior, *Założenia autorskie*, "Architektura-Murator" 2005, 10 (133), pp. 44–46, as well as a lecture given by the designer at the Faculty of Architecture of the Silesian University of Technology in 2004.

55 E. Kuryłowicz, *Wydział Neofilologii UW. Założenia autorskie*, "Architektura-Murator" 2013, no 04 (223), pp. 66–71.

56 K. Gronkiewicz, *Wydział Neofilologii UW*, "Architektura-Murator" 2013, no. 04 (223), pp. 62–66.

57 N. Juzwa, J. Świerzawski, Concept of surface curvature versus a smooth box in architecture, in: *What's the Matter? Materiality and Materialism at the Age of Computation*, ed. M. Voyatzaki, Barcelona 2014.

58 http://hs99.pl/2002-katowice-academic-library [access: 10.08.2014].

59 *Historia*, www.bracz.edu.pl/o-bibliotece/o-instytucji/historia/ [access: 20.09.2019].

60 T. Malkowski, *Biblioteka Raczyńskich*, in: *Form Follows Freedom . . .*, pp. 82–91, and *Marek Moskal, Jerzy Szczepanik-Dzikowski in an interview for Strefa Przestrzeni*, www.youtube.com/watch?v=iNnDwEqu6o8 [access: 20.09.2019].

61 C. Wąs, *Bunt kwiatu przeciw korzeniom. Polska architektura sakralna lat 1980–2005 wobec modernizmu*, "Quart" 2006, no. 1, pp. 74–87.

62 See: W. Bonowicz, *Samolot, gołębica i Matka Boża*, www.wniebowstapienie.pl/parafia/historia/ [access: 28.10.2019].

63 *Gont i Beton*, www.bryla.pl/bryla/1,85298,6756638,Gont_i_Beton.html [access: 13.09.2019].

64 *Wooden Church*, https://miesarch.com/work/2087 [access: 13.09.2019].

65 W. Bochenek, *Nowy budynek wpisany do mazowieckiego rejestu zabytków – ma tylko 11 lat!*, "Architektura i biznes" 06.12.2022, www.architekturaibiznes.pl/nowy-zabytek-w-mazowieckim-rejestrze-ma-tylko-11-lat,14922.html [access: 22.01.2023].

Conclusion

Architecture and Art

In concluding our thoughts on architecture in innovative contemporaneity, it would be fitting to end with a response to the question on the relations between architecture and art. The question appears in various discussions, providing many, sometimes contradictory answers and combining with a question: What is architecture in the contemporary world? Certainly, it is one of the oldest records about our life and its history. Despite the trends of contemporary development, the physicality of architecture continually persists. Architecture surrounds us with its massiveness, protecting our lives and our actions – it is always around us. In the past, it was the domain of kings and the wealthy; today, in the times of mature capitalism, it requires a business plan.

Although architecture is often created thanks to the idea of a single person, in order to exist in the real world, it requires the effort of many. Moreover, it does not come into existence until there is a need for it, until somebody pays the bills. Although it is one of the most expensive activities ever invented by man,[1] it continues to be created, while the prices of the designed/implemented buildings constantly increase.

As we have said, the creation of architecture is a business that requires the collaboration of numerous groups of people. This feature results in architecture being ranked the lowest among all other fields that make up art.[2]

The book *The Art Instinct: Beauty, Pleasure, and the Human Evolution* lists 12 criteria that make up the characteristics of a work of art or which make up the quality of the experience of art. It seems that these criteria are equally important for architecture. According to Denis Dutton,[3] these are:

- **Direct pleasure.** Taking pleasure from artistic beauty (the object) is a source of pleasure in itself. We often speak of pleasure "in itself." In such an experience, the most important fact is that it comes from multi-layered

DOI: 10.4324/9781003413561-5

pleasures, with distinguishable variety and diversity. Such multi-layered experiences are best experienced when they interact with one another.
- **Skill and virtuosity.** Creating a work of art is based on practicing virtuosity in a certain specialized field. Virtuosity does not concern solely art. It occurs in various fields; therefore, it is not only intellectual admiration for skills. Virtuosity, which is a source of pleasure, is one of the most moving aspects of art.
- **Style** outlines the framework, within which the artist creates the form, composition, or expression of the work. Dutton[4] writes that style may overburden the artist, but more often than not, it liberates him. The style creates the framework within which the artist can bestow individual characteristics upon his works.
- **Novelty and creativity.** *Creativity* means the ability to attract attention, but also the artist's aptness in discovering new meanings in relation to the subject undertaken or to the substance used to create the piece. These traits are a place where the artistic individuality is not driven by any specific rules or procedures, expressing the artistic individuality or even ingeniousness of the artist.
- **Criticism.** Wherever there are art forms, there is also criticism. Professional criticism, for example, in academic education, is a kind of a spectacle, but also the object of evaluation of a broader audience.
- **Representation.** Taking on various ranges of perspective, various perspectives, works of art imitate, and sometimes represent, the real or imagined experience of the world. The author notices the sense of works that imitate and whose significance is expressed indirectly.
- **Special focus.** Works of art, as well as artistic spectacles, seem to exist outside the boundaries of ordinary life. They create experiences "for their own sake" – a feature that is clearly articulated in the works of Gadamer. It is also reminiscent of the words of Ellen Dissanayake, who talks about "bestowing a specific character upon things, arousing exceptionality,"[5] which can be expressed in various ways.
- **Expressive individuality.** It is often important in fields in which that which is included in creativity is defined in a loose or even an ambiguous way. This occurs in relation to activities where it is important to express individuality.
- **Emotional saturation.** Interacting with a work of art is generally connected with experiencing a certain emotional state. Dutton divides such emotions into two different kinds. The first is emotions which we experience in everyday life, such as fear, joy, surprise. The second is generally recorded as a unique emotional contour of an artwork. Invoking the works of Duchamp,[6] Dutton notices that an object whose main feature is neutrality or universality, shown as a work of art, is connected with experiencing an emotional state.

Conclusion 177

- **Intellectual challenge.** The task of a work of art is to put our minds into a state of intellectual excitement while also enabling the interpretation of sensual impressions. We may speak of invoking conceptual or artistic relations that a given object brings to mind; an idea can also be discovered in the words of architect-designers quoted in the part "Continuity of Thought in Architecture."
- **Art traditions and institutions.** Structures, as well as artistic spectacles, are created within the framework of existing historical traditions. This statement complies with the thought of Jerrold Levinson,[7] who says that works of art acquire their identity in compliance with the historical tradition, which is a testimony of their recognition. This feature does not apply to the so-called art canon, such as Beethoven's *IX Symphony* or Michelangelo's *Pietà*. A similar truth is noticed by Anda Rottenberg when she speaks of beauty that requires understanding, but also universalization. She reminds us that only then is an object accepted and seen as beautiful.
- **Imaginative experience.** On this list, imagination is the most important determinant or criterion of art. The artistic experience takes place in a "theater of the imagination." It is not only a beautiful statement but also a very important one, because it clearly separates the imagination from practical matters. It liberates it from the limitations of logic and rationality. For Kant, works of art are the creative objects of selfless contemplation. In this sense, we might have said that many of them are expressed in a world of appearances.[8]

In speaking of a theater of the imagination, which seems to be the most important event in the creation of a work of art, we may confirm its significance, especially in the process of creating an idea. Nevertheless, for architecture to be created, this justified list should be enriched by another list, this one more pragmatic in character. In its relations, the list reaches all the way to questions of construction, of the technology of the architectural material, and finally, these stemming from the sphere of social issues or environmental protection, to name only the most important ones.

Architecture is an autonomous field that is strongly connected with art and culture. Such statements can be heard in the words of the laureates of the Pritzker Award, compiled in a study by Ruth Peltason and Grace Ong-Yan, titled *Architect: The Pritzker Prize Laureates in Their Own Words*.[9]

Along with Aristotle, we may say that we are born as image-makers and image-enthusiasts. From the times of this ancient philosopher, we value understanding of autonomous integrality and diversity of the arts. It does not contradict another, equally old thought that speaks of tensions existing between the cultural tradition and the natural world. Dutton also reminds us that human fate is part of the physical world – the natural one.

Figure 4.1 The Chopin Center in Warsaw, Bolesław Stelmach, Stelmach & Partners Architectural Office, 2010.

Source: Marcin Czechowicz/Stelmach & Partners Architectural Office.

Conclusion 179

If, according to yet another prominent figure of the ancient world, Plato, art is immutably illusory, since it is a representation of the "imitation of eternal forms," then, according to Aristotle, art is a kind of a combination of general laws and human emotions. The connection that imitates human emotions is present both in melody as well as in rhythm. It is distinctly visible in fields that use words, marble, or paint,[10] but it also occurs in contemporary architecture, which utilizes computers to express architectural beauty.

Architecture is an autonomous field, drawing knowledge inspiration, creativity from other fields, including art. Similar reflections are present in the statements of architect-creators whom we have quoted earlier in our work, but also in the statements of architects whom we have "invited" to sum up our work.

Tomasz Konior, in recalling the problem of complexity in the process of shaping and implementing architecture, says:

The architect invariably tries to meet the expectations of the investor. At the same time, he strives to remain faithful to the universal values and his own convictions . . . collaborates with an ever-growing group of engineers and experts. The tasks put in front of him often lead to difficult choices as well as questions on where to draw the line of compromise. As far as the public is concerned it is still the architect, although often thoroughly undeservingly who is responsible for the final effect.[11]

These words are echoed by Helmut Jahn, who, in describing his own activities, not without reason, calls upon a musical metaphor:

You must be sure that you are creating the proper tones, that the building will play like music, that it will sound appropriate, it cannot simply fill up space, it must be recognizable. Signs of these are distinct form, taking care of colors, blurring the borders between public and private space, buildings, which react to the urban space with composition and rhythm.[12]

In comparison with text, painting, and music, architecture is a less-precise form of expression. However, at the same time, for a building to be created, an enormous joint effort is required. We employ others to create the environment in which we live and work. Moreover, we would like for the environment created around us to speak.

All these desires and thoughts come together in a definition stating that architecture is an autonomous creation that serves people. It is created to bring joy to human eyes, losing its value when the utility value of the building is degraded. This truth most fully expresses itself in the never-ending drive to create functional perfection as well as in maintaining faith in the beauty of the created buildings.

Notes

1. T. Dyckhoff, *The Age of Spectacle* . . ., p. 21.
2. G.W.F. Hegel, *Hegel's Aesthetics: Lectures Fine Art*, Vol. 2, Oxford 1975, pp. 82–85, see: T. Dyckhoff, *The Age of Spectacle* . . .
3. D. Dutton, *The Art. Instinct* . . . We used content from chapter 3 titled: *What is Art*.
4. D. Dutton, *The Art. Instinct* . . ., p. 103.
5. Ibid., p. 106.
6. A reference to a discussion about Duchamp exhibiting a urinal as a work of art. This began a discussion in literature; ready-made items, produced earlier, cannot express originality such as a painting can, but they can be a pretext for interpretation, provoking discussion regarding art and its presentation.
7. D. Dutton, *The Art. Instinct* . . ., p. 110.
8. In our thoughts on the criteria important for the definition of what is art., we used Chapter 3 from D. Dutton's *The Art Instinct* . . ., pp. 93–119, pp. 313–336.
9. R. Peltason, G. Ong-Yan, *Pritzker Prize Laureates* . . .
10. D. Dutton, *The Art Instinct* . . ., pp. 71–76.
11. Tomasz Konior in an interview with Jerzy Ziemiacki: J. Ziemacki, *Architektura to nie tylko budynki,* "Rzeczpospolita", 27.12.2019, https://www.rp.pl/nieruchomosci/art965591-architektura-to-nie-tylko-budynki [access: 27.06.2021].
12. *Światowej sławy architekt odebrał nagrodę za warszawski projekt,* www.nationalgeographic.pl/ludzie/swiatowej-slawy-architekt-helmut-jahn-odebral-nagrode-zawarszawski-projekt-to-wyjatkowy-wklad-w-urbanistyczny-pejzaz-stolicy [access: 15.11.2019].

Bibliography

Non-Serial Publications

Ackermann J., *Origins, Imitation, Conventions. Representation in the Visual Arts*, Cambridge 2001.
Architect. The Pritzker Prize Laureates in Their Own Words, eds. R. Peltason Ruth, G. Ong-Yan Grace, London 2010.
Battistini M., *Symbole i alegorie*, Warsaw 2005.
Basista A., *Wartość i architektura*, Cracow 2005.
Bauman Z., *Płynna nowoczesność*, Cracow 2006.
Bonenberg A., *Media, przestrzeń, architektura. Transformacje przestrzeni społeczeństwa informacyjnego*, Poznan 2013.
Burry J., Burry M., *The New Mathematics of Architecture*, London 2012.
Le Cahiers de l'enseignement de l'architecture, no. 5, ed. M. Voyatzaki, Thessaloniki 1999.
Les Cahiers de l'enseignement de l'architecture, no. 9, ed. S. Hano.ot, *Entre l'architecte et l'ingenieur. L'enseignement a la recherche d'une pratique pluridisiplinaire*, Paris 2000.
Dekalog dobrej przestrzeni, eds. M. Szczelina, A. Ostrowska, Katowice 2019.
Dutton D., *Instynkt sztuki. Piękno, zachwyt i ewolucja człowieka*, transl. by J. Luty, Cracow 2019.
Dyckhoff T., *Epoka spektaklu. Perypetie miasta i architektury XX wieku*, transl. by A. Rasmus-Zgorzelska, Cracow 2018.
Emmer M., *Architecture and Mathematics. Soap Bubbles and Soap Films, w: Architecture and Mathematics from Antiquity to the Future*, Vol. 2, eds. K. Williams, M.J. Ostwald, Cham 2015, pp. 454–455.
Fischer G., *Architekturtheorie für Architekten. Die theoretischen Grundlagen des Faches Architektur*, Basel 2014.
Form Follows Freedom. Architektura dla kultury w Polsce 2000, ed. J. Purchla, J. Sepioł, Cracow 2015.
Gadamer H.-G., *Aktualność piękna. Sztuka jako gra, symbol i święto*, Warsaw 1993.
Gadamer H.-G., *Prawda i metoda*, Warsaw 2004.
Gawell E., *Non-Euclidean Geometry in the Modelling of Contemporary Architectural Forms*, "The Journal of Polish Society for Geometry and Engineering Graphics" 2013, no. 24.
Gehl J., *Życie między budynkami*, Cracow 2009.

182 Bibliography

Gehl J., *Miasto dla ludzi*, Cracow 2014.
Gelernter M., *Sources of Architectural Form. A Critical History of Western Design Theory*, Manchester and New York 1995.
Gössel P., Leuthäuser G., *Architektura XX wieku*, transl. by K. Frankowska, L. Głuchowska, Köln 2010.
Goldberger P., *Building Art. The Life and Work of Frank Gehry*, New York 2015.
de Graaf R., *Cztery ściany i dach*, transl. by G. Piątek, Warsaw-Cracow 2019.
Graham W., *Miasta wyśnione*, transl. by A. Sak, Cracow 2016.
Gropius W., *Pełnia architektury*, transl. by K. Kopczyńska, Cracow 2014.
Harbison R., *Zbudowane, niezbudowane i nie do zbudowania*, Warsaw 2001.
Historia piękna, ed. U. Eco, transl. by A. Kusiak, Poznan 2005.
Ingarden R., *O dziele architektury, w: Studia z estetyki*, Vol. 2, Warsaw 1966.
Jałowiecki B., *Miejsce, przestrzeń, obszar*, "Przegląd Socjologiczny" 2011, no. 60.
Jencks Ch., *Le Corbusier – tragizm współczesnej architektury*, transl. by M. Biegańska, Warsaw 1982.
Jencks Ch., *Ruch nowoczesny w architekturze*, tłum. A. Morawińska, H Pawlikowska, Warsaw 1987.
Jencks Ch., *The Architecture of the Jumping Universe a Polemic: How Complexity Science is Changing Architecture and Culture*, Chichester, London 1995.
Jencks Ch., *Extatic Architecture. The Surprising Link*, New York 1999.
Jencks Ch., *The Iconic Building*, New York 2005.
Jodidio Ph., *Sir Norman Foster*, Köln 2001.
Jodidio Ph., *Hadid. Complete Works 1979–2013*, Köln 2013.
Juzwa N., *Marketing i medialność "nowej" architektury, przykład obiektu przemysłowego*, "Czasopismo Techniczne" 2010, r. 107, J. 7.
Juzwa N., *Moje domy w Nowym Jorku*, in: *Dom w mieście: właściwości rzeczy architektonicznej*, ed. D. Kozłowski, Czasopismo Techniczne, Vol. 1, Cracow 2016.
Juzwa N., Pragmatism or emotion? The sources of architectural form, in: *Defining the Architectural Space: Rationalistic or Intuitive Way to Architecture: Monograph. Vol. 1 = Definiowanie przestrzeni architektonicznej: racjonalistyczna czy intuicyjna droga do architektury: monografia. Vol. 1*, ed. T. Kozłowski, Cracow 2018.
Juzwa N., The beauty in architecture, in: *Defining the Architectural Space – Tradition and Modernity in Architecture. Vol. 1*, ed. W. Celadyn, Cracow 2019.
Juzwa N., Gil A., *Współczesne postrzeganie architektury: idea, obiekt, tworzywo*, "Czasopismo Techniczne" 2006, vol. 103, J. 9.
Juzwa N., Gil A., Sulimowska A., Witeczek A., *Architecture and Urban Planning for Contemporary Industry*, Gliwice 2016.
Juzwa N., Gil A., Ujma-Wąsowicz K., Almost human architecture, examples of polish architecture, where the a human factor co-created the architectural concept, in: *Ergonomics and Environmental Design*, Los Angeles 2015.
Juzwa N., Gil A., Ujma-Wąsowicz K., *Does Computer Have Control Over an Architect. Some Reflection on Example of Sports Arenas, w: Universal Access in Computer Interaction*, eds. M. Antona, C. Stephanides, Los Angeles 2015.
Juzwa N., Gil A., Ujma-Wąsowicz K., Innovation of modern architecture – expressionist tendencies, in: *Advances in Physical Ergonomics and Human Factors*, eds. R.S. Goonetilleke, W. Karwowski, Springer, Cham 2016.
Juzwa N., Krotowski T., Sketch – computer – imagination, in: *Computing for a Better Tomorrow*, Łódź 2018.

Bibliography 183

Juzwa N., Krotowski T., High habitats – do we like high? in: *Theory of Habitat. Contemporary Context*, Warsaw 2019.

Juzwa N., Świerzawski J., Concept of surface curvature versus a smooth box in architecture in: *What's the Matter? Materiality and Materialism at the Age of Computation*, ed. M. Voyatzaki, Barcelona 2014.

Juzwa N., Świerzawski J., Facades – A magnificent falsehood of architecture, in: *Defining The Architectural Sace – The Truth and Lie of Architecture*, Vol. 1, ed. W. Celadyn, Cracow 2020.

Juzwa N., Ujma-Wąsowicz K., Large scale Architecture – does new architectural geometry require a reinspection of comfortable usage and the users emotions? in: *Proceedings 4th International Conference on Applied Human Factors and Ergonomics*, San Francisco 2012.

Kołakowski L., *Mini wykłady o maxi sprawach*, Cracow 2004.

Kozłowski T., *Tendencje ekspresjonistyczne w architekturze współczesnej*, Cracow 2013.

Kozłowski T., *Architektura a sztuka*, Cracow 2018.

Koolhaas R., *Deliryczny Nowy Jork*, Cracow 2013.

Kuhn R., Juzwa N., Luciani D., *Landschffen Verwandeln*, published in German, Italian, Polish, and English, Berlin 2006.

Meissner I., Möller E., Otto F., *Forschen, Bauen, Inspirieren*, München 2015, pp. 9–34.

Misiągiewicz M., *O prezentacji idei architektonicznej*, Cracow 2003.

Moderne Architektur A – Z, Vol. 2, ed. P. Gössel, Köln 2007.

Monestiroli A., *Tryglif i metopa*, Cracow 2009.

Otterbeck J., *Oslo Opera House*, Oslo 2009.

Palus K., *Architektura sakralna regionu Podhala. Tradycja i nowoczesność*, Gliwice 2011.

Pinson D., *Des banlieues et des villes*, Paris 1992.

Rogers E.M., *Diffusion of Innovation*, New York 2010.

Rumińska A., *101 najciekawszych polskich budynków dekady*, Warsaw 2011.

du Sautoy M., *Kod kreatywności. Sztuka i innowacje w epoce sztucznej inteligencji*, transl. by T. Chawziuk, Cracow 2020.

Schoen D.A., *The Reflective Practitioner. How Professionals Think in Action*, London 1983.

Siegel C., *Formy strukturalne w nowoczesnej architekturze*, transl. by E. Piliszek, Warsaw 1964.

Słyk J., *Źródła architektury informacyjnej*, Warsaw 2012.

Słyk J., *Modele architektoniczne*, Warsaw 2019.

Świerzawski J., Przemiana, in: *Tożsamość. 100 lat polskiej architektury*, eds. B. Stelmach, K. Batko-Andrzejewska, Warsaw 2019.

Tatarkiewicz Wł., *Dzieje sześciu pojęć*, Warsaw 1975.

Tatarkiewicz Wł., *O doskonałości. Wybrane eseje*, Warsaw 1976.

Tożsamość. 100 lat polskiej architektury, eds. B. Stelmach, K. Andrzejewska-Batko, Warsaw 2019.

Tschumi B., *Event-Cities 3. Concept vs. Context vs. Content*, London 2005.

Tschumi B., *Event-Cities 4. Concept-Form*, London 2010.

Tuan Y.-F., *Przestrzeń i miejsce*, transl. by A. Morawińska, Warsaw 1987.

Tulkowska-Słyk K., *Nowoczesne mieszkanie*, Warsaw 2019.

Węcławik P., *Antropologia filozoficzna Maxa Schelera. Jej geneza, przedmiot i metoda*, "Folia Philosophica" 1998, vol. 16.

Węcławowicz-Gyurkovich E., *Architektura najnowsza w środowisku miast historycznych*, Cracow 2013.
Weston R., *Plans, Sections and Elevations. Key Buildings of The Twentieth Century*, Londyn 2004.
Winskowski P., *Modernizm przebudowany*, Cracow 2000.
Witruwiusz, *O Architekturze ksiąg dziesięć*, tłum. K. Kumaniecki, Warsaw 1999.
Wright F.L., *Architektura nowoczesna. Wykłady*, tłum. D. Żukowski, Cracow 2016.
Lewis P., Tsurumaki M., Lewis D.J., *Manual of Section*, New York 2016.

Magazines

1. Znak. *Miesięcznik*, "wrzesień" 2016, no. 736, pp. 74–87.
2. *Architektura kontekstu. Z architektami Andrzejem Bulandą i Włodzimierzem Muchą, właścicielami pracowni Balanda & Mucha Architekci, rozmawia Teodor Wernicki*, "Sto Journal" 2007, no. 1, r. 11, p. 2.
3. Budzyński M., Badowski Z., *Założenia autorskie*, "Architektura-Murator" 2000, no. 1, p. 28.
4. Budzyński M., *Walka o osiągnięcie jedni*, "Architektura-Murator" 2012, no. 11, p. 60.
5. Czupkiewicz A., *Siedziba MPWiK we Wrocławiu*, "Architektura-Murator" 2019, no. 7, pp. 48–54.
6. Dziewoński M., *Założenia projektowe*, "Architektura-Murator" 2019, no. 7, p. 49.
7. Fernando Marquez C., Levene R., *Jean Nouvel 2007–2016 Contemporary Reflections*, "El Croquis" 2016, no. 183, p. 242.
8. Gronkiewicz K., *Wydział Neofilologii UW*, "Architektura-Murator" 2013, no. 4, pp. 62–66.
9. Hauberg J., *Research by Design – a Research Strategy*, "Architecture & Education Journal" 2011, no. 5, pp. 46–56.
10. Ingarden K., *Założenia autorskie*, "Architektura-Murator" 2013, no. 4, pp. 44–45.
11. Konior T., *Założenia autorskie*, "Architektura-Murator" 2005, no. 10, pp. 44–46.
12. Kozłowski D., *Beton i mistrzowie transmutacji materii*, "Pretekst" 2018, no. 8, p. 70.
13. Kuryłowicz E., *Wydział Neofilologii UW. Założenia autorskie*, "Architektura-Murator" 2013, no. 4, pp. 66–71.
14. *Lista przebojów*, "Architektura-Murator" 1997, no. 10 (37), p. 14.
15. Loegler R., *Założenia projektowe*, "Architektura-Murator" 2004, no. 12, p. 51.
16. Majewski J.S., *Giełda*, "Architektura-Murator" 2000, no. 9, pp. 32–40.
17. Malkowski T., *Ceglana melodia*, "Architektura i Biznes" 2008, no. 6, p. 64.
18. Michalak T., *Teatr otwarty*, "Architektura-Murator" 2016, no. 8, pp. 64–65.
19. Miłobędzki M., *Nastrój kreowany światłem*, "Architektura-Murator" 2014, no. 7, p. 52.
20. Mycielski K., *Wieżowiec Q22 w Warszawie*, "Architektura Murator" 2017, no. 2, pp. 56–62.
21. *Nominacje do nagród głównych*, "Architektura-Murator" 2013, no. 2 (221), p. 43.
22. Oleksiak J., *Rozmowa z Fernando Menisem*, "Architektura i Biznes" 2009, no. 10, p. 80.
23. Przestaszewska-Porębska E., *Nagroda Roku Stowarzyszenia Architektów Polskich SARP 1983*, "Architektura" 1985, no. 3, pp. 65–71.

24. *Sąd Najwyższy*, "Architektura-Murator" 2000, no. 1 (64), pp. 12–22.
25. Stiasny G., *Agora*, "Architektura-Murator" 2002, no. 5, pp. 9–18.
26. Stiasny G., *Od A Do Z – Alfabet Architektury*, "Architektura-Murator" 2004, no. 10, p. 110.
27. Stiasny G., *Szkoła w Białołęce*, "Architektura-Murator" 2005, no. 10, pp. 42–44.
28. Stiasny G., *Wydział Finansów w Krakowie*, "Architektura-Murator" 2004, no. 12, 46–50.
29. Szczepanik-Dzikowski J., *Założenia autorskie*, "Architektura-Murator" 2002, no. 5, pp. 25–27.
30. Wąs C., *Bunt kwiatu przeciw korzeniom. Polska architektura sakralna lat 1980–2005 wobec modernizmu*, "Quart" 2006, no. 1, pp. 74–87.

PhD Dissertations

- Konior T., *Ewolucja przestrzeni publicznej w budynkach dla muzyki. Koncept. Kontekst. Architektura*, doctoral student, thesis supervisor: N. Juzwa, Łódź University of Technolgy 2019.
- Krotowski T., *Ewolucja ściany osłonowej na przykładzie pawilonów EXPO*, doctoral student, thesis supervisor: N. Juzwa, Łódź University of Technology 2016.
- Świerzawski J., *Krzywoliniowość w architekturze. Historia. Współczesność. Idee. Przykłady*, doctoral student, thesis supervisor: N. Juzwa, Łódź University of Technology 2017.

Electronic Publications

- Bochenek W., *Nowy budynek wpisany do mazowieckiego rejestu zabytków – ma tylko 11 lat!*, "Architektura i biznes" 06.12.2022, www.architekturaibiznes.pl/nowy-zabytek-w-mazowieckim-rejestrze-ma-tylko-11-lat,14922.html [access: 22.01.2023].
- Brzechwa J., *Mrówka*, http://wiersze.kobieta.pl/wiersz/jan-brzechwa/mrowka-165 [access: 15.09.2020].
- *Nominacje do nagrody im. Miesa van der Rohe 2019 – Muzeum II Wojny Światowej w Gdańsku*, archinea.pl/nominacje-do-nagrody-im-miesa-van-der-rohe-2019-muzeum-ii-wojny-swiatowej-w-gdansku/ [access: 16.12.2019].
- *Jan Kubec w rozmowie z Tomaszem Malkowskim*, archirama.muratorplus.pl/architektura/jan-kubec-architekt-centrum-nauki-kopernik-opowiada-o-swojej-nowatorskiej-architekturze,67_1317.html?&page=1 [access: 13.09.2019].
- Zumthor P., *Personal Interview with Edward Lifson for His Blog*, architecturalinterviews.blogspot.com/2009/12/peter-dzumthor-personal-interview-with.html [access: 15.03.2019].
- *Budynek BRE Banku w Bydgoszczy*, architektura.muratorplus.pl/kolekcja-architektury/budynek-bre-banku-w-bydgoszczy_3726.html [access: 04.09.2019].
- Pięciak P., *Wierzę w ludzi i marzę . . .*, architekturabetonowa.pl/aktualności/1060/wierze-w-ludzi-i-marze [access: 27.12.2019].
- Pięciak P., *W świecie fikcji, opery, wspaniałego kłamstwa i betonu*, architekturabetonowa.pl/aktualności/1257/wświecie-fikcji-opery-wspaniałego-kłamstwa-i-betonu/ [access: 13.12.2019].

186 Bibliography

- *Historia*, www.bracz.edu.pl/o-bibliotece/o-instytucji/historia/ [access: 20.09.2019].
- *Muzeum z pudełek*, Bryła.pl/bryła/1,85298,464640,muzeum-z-pudełek.html [access: 27.12.2019].
- *OMA rozbuduje Muzeum Sztuki Współczesnej w Nowym Jorku*, Bryła.pl/bryła/7,85-298,2497855,oma-rozbudowuje-nowe-muzeum-sztuki-wspolczesnej-w-nowym-jorku [access: 27.12.2019].
- *Bałtyk Tower. Innowacyjność i wizja*, builderpolska.pl/2017/10/02/bałtyk-towe-innowacyjność-i-wizja/ [access: 15.12.19].
- *Budowa Muzeum Tadeusz Kantora i nowej siedziby CRICOTEKI*, cricotekawbudowie.pl/pl,dokumentacja-fotograficzna [access: 19.09.2019].
- Cymer A., *Łódzkie fabryki wczoraj i dziś*, culture.pl/pl/artykul/lodzkie-fabryki-wczoraj-i-dzis [access: 9.12.2019].
- Klein L., Duda A., *Marek Budzyński*, culture.pl/pl/tworca/marek-budzynski [access: 28.10.2019].
- hs99.pl/2002-katowice-academic-library [access: 10.08.2014].
- Stangel M., *Miasta dla ludzi – an interview with Jan Gehl*, http://arcastangel.pl/miasta-dla-ludzi-rozmowa-z-janem-gehlem/ [access: 2.02.2020].
- http://jems.pl/onas/ [access: 18.03.2019].
- *Hala Koszyki*, http://jems.pl/projekty/wszystkie-prace/hala-koszyki.htm [access: 20.09.2019].
- Juzwa N., Gil A., Ujma-Wąsowicz K., *Almost Human Architecture*, http://kaiu.pan.pl/index.php?option=com_content&view=article&id=463&catid=60&Itemid=56 [access: 3.10.2019].
- Konior T., in *an interview with Jerzy Ziemiacki*: J. Ziemacki, *Architektura to nie tylko budynki*, "Rzeczpospolita", 27.12.2019, https://www.rp.pl/nieruchomosci/art965591-architektura-to-nie-tylko-budynki [access: 27.06.2021].
- Kopia B., *Muzeum Miejskie w Tychach*, http://muzeum.tychy.pl/zbiory/fotografia/zygmunt-wieczorek/ [access: 24.09.2019].
- Piotrowski M., *La Tourette, czyli co betonowy klasztor mówi o modernizmie*, http://onowymodernizm.pl/la-tourette [access: 17.08.2018].
- *Le Rolex Center*, http://rolexlearningcenter.epfl.ch/ [access: 19.12.2014].
- Piątek G., *Co architektura mówi o Polakach*, http://wyborcza.pl/1,75410,16742445,Co_architektura_mowi_o_Polakach.html [access: 17.10.2019].
- *Centrum Spotkania Kultur w Lublinie*, https://architektura.info/architektura/polska_i_swiat/centrum_spotkania_kultur_w_lublinie [access: 18.11.2019].
- Mozga-Górecka M., *Zawód architekt: Dariusz Kozłowski*, https://architektura.muratorplus.pl/architektura25/zawod-architekt-dariusz-kozlowski_3886.html [access: 18.03.2019].
- *Centrum Spotkania Kultur*, https://culture.pl/pl/dzielo/centrum-spotkania-kultur [access: 20.11.2019].
- Mróz M., *Popchnąć świat do przodu – Helmut Jahn i jego klasyczny modernizm*, https://internityhome.pl/ih4/popchnac-swiat-przodu-helmut-jahn-klasyczny-modernizm/ [access: 5.01.2020].
- Kuma K. et al., *LVMH Osaka*, https://kkaa.co.jp/works/architecture/lvmh-osaka/ [access: 28.11.2019].
- https://nyc-architecture.com/UES/UES080.htm [access: 15.04.2020].
- https://opoka.org.pl/biblioteka/I/IS/polskie_koscioly.html [access: 28.10.2019].

Bibliography 187

- Stec B., *Wyższe Seminarium Duchowne Księży Zmartwychwstańców Centrum Resurrectionis*, https://pomoszlak.pl/seminarium-zmartwychwstancow/ [access: 20.11.2019].
- Mróz M., *Uczynić świat lepszym – an interview with Helmut Jahn*, https://sztuka-architektury.pl/article/4745/8222uczynic-swiat-lepszym8221-wywiad-z-helmutem-jahn-em [access: 15.03.2019].
- Kozanecki P., Paturej B., *Tomasz Konior. Dziecko modernizmu w potrzasku*, https://wiadomosci.onet.pl/tylko-w-onecie/tomasz-konior-dziecko-modernizmu-w-potrzasku-wywiad/5devzd [access: 15.05.2019].
- Sveiven M., *AD Classics. Sendai Mediatheque/Toyo Ito & Associates*, www.archdaily.com/118627/ad-classics-sendai-mediatheque-toyo-ito [access: 8.05.2018].
- *The Therme Vals/Peter Zumthor*, www.archdaily.com/13358/the-therme-vals [access: 30.08.2019].
- Blundell Jones P., *Parc de La Villette in Paris, France, by Bernard Tschumi*, www.architectural-review.com/buildings/parc-de-la-villette-in-paris-france-by-bernard-tschumi/8630513.article [access: 5.04.2019].
- *Europejskie Centrum Solidarności*, www.bryla.pl/bryla/1,85301,16504373,Europejskie_Centrum_Solidarnosci_w_Gdansku__ZDJECIA_.html [access: 15.10.2019].
- *Biblioteka Uniwersytecka w Warszawie, Budynek i ogród*, www.buw.uw.edu.pl/o-nas/budynek-i-ogrod/ [access: 17.10.2019].
- Goldberger P., *Swiss Mystique*, www.vanity fair.com/peter-zumthor-architect-buildings [access: 12.06.2019].
- *Historia budowy Centrum*, jordanki.torun.pl/budowa/ [access: 31.12.2019].
- Lewicki P., Łatak K., *O hali*, karcherhalacracovia.pl/o-hali/ [access: 27.12.2019].
- *O parku*, lpnt.pl/ [access: 28.11.2019].
- menis.es/en/portfolio/centro-de-cultura-y-congresos-ckk-jordanki/ [access: 14.09.2019].
- *District Court in Katowice*, miesarch.com/work/1999 [access: 19.09.2019].
- *Wooden Church*, miesarch.com/work/2087 [access: 13.09.2019].
- *Jordanki Culture and Congress Centre, CKK*, "Jordanki", miesarch.com/work/3658 [access: 14.09.2019].
- *The Regional Court Building Complex in Siedlce*, miesarch.com/work/3731 [access: 19.09.2019].
- *Cracovia 1906 Centennial Hall with the Sports Center for the Handicapped*, miesarch.com/work/3824 [access: 27.12.2019].
- *Bałtyk office building*, miesarch.com/work/3927 [access: 18.09.2019].
- *The Copernicus Science Centre*, miesarch.com/work/441 [access: 13.09.2019].
- *The Chopin Center*, miesarch.com/work/493 [access: 03.10.2019].
- *Museum of Polish Aviation*, https://miesarch.com/work/459 [access: 3.12.2019].
- *Philharmonic Hall*, www.miesarch.com/work/567 [access: 18.09.2019].
- *Sanktuarium MB Objawiającej Cudowny Medalik. Księża Misjonarze św. Wincentego a Paulo*, misjonarze-zakopane.pl/index.php/nowy-kocio/ [access: 30.10.2019].
- *Budynek Sądu Okręgowego*, npp.slaskie.pl/vote/content/edition_5_project_130 [access: 19.09.2019].
- *O nas*, penderecki-center.pl/o-nas [access: 06.12.2019].
- Łujaszewski J., *Bałtyk najlepszym budynkiem roku w Poznaniu. Nagroda Quadro pierwszy raz dla cudzoziemca: 300 makiet i kilka lat prób*, poznan.wyborcza.pl/poznan/7,36001,24054188,300-makiet-i-kilka-lat-prob-nagroda-quadro-po-raz-pierwszy.html [access: 18.09.2019].

188 Bibliography

- rolexlearningcenter.epfl.ch/files/content/sites/rolexlearningcenter/files/press%20kit/ ENGLISH%20Kit2012.pdf [access: 25.09.2015].
- Sołoducha K., *Życie na trzech poziomach – wywiad*, sztuka-architektury.pl/article/ 10301/muzeum-drugiej-wojny-zycia-na-trzech-poziomach [access: 03.10.2019].
- ICHOT. *Brama Poznania z nagrodą Jana Baptysty Quadro*, sztuka-architektury. pl/article/2953/ichot-brama-poznania-z-nagroda-jana-baptysty-quadro [access: 16.12.2019].
- *Do środka*, sztuka-architektury.pl/article/3631/do-srodka [access: 23.09.2019].
- *Zanurzony w życiu*, sztuka-architektury.pl/article/3665/zanurzony-w-zyciu [access: 3.10.2019].
- Cymer A., *Szekspir zamieszka w Gdańsku*, sztuka-architektury.pl/article/4541/ szekspir-zamieszka-w-gdansku [access: 24.09.2019].
- Tschumi B., *Event Cities 3: Concept vs. Content*, London 2005, teoriaarchitektury. blogspot.com/2013/08/bernard-tschumi-concept-context-content [access: 28.08.2019].
- *Toruń z zeszłym roku odwiedziło aż 2,35 mln turystów*, torun.wyborcza.pl/ torun/7,48723,24699545,torun-odwiedzilo-w-zeszlym-roku-az-2-mln-turystow. html [access: 14.09.2019].
- *Hotel u Kennedy'ego*, Tvn24bis.pl/wiadomości-gospodarcze,74/hotel-u-kennedyego,161294.html [access: 15.04.2020].
- Kuryłowicz & Associates, *Focus*, www.apaka.com.pl/pl/projekty/budynek-biurowyfokus [access: 3.10.2019].
- Kuryłowicz & Associates, *Q22*, www.apaka.com.pl/pl/publikacje/wiezowiecq22-w-warszawie [access: 30.10.2019].
- Kroll A., *AD Classics: Munich Olympic Stadium/Frei Otto & Gunther Behnisch*, www.archdaily.com/?p=109136 [access: 10.11.2014].
- Jordana S., *Interview: Robert Venturi & Denise Brown Scott, by Andrea Tamas*, www.archdaily.com/130389/interview-robert-venturi-denise-scott-brown-byandrea-tamas [access: 27.03.2019].
- *Rolex Learning Center/SANAA*, www.archdaily.com/50235/ [access: 19.12.2014].
- *Science and Musical Education Center Symphony/Konior Studio*, www.archdaily. com/511867/science-and-musical-education-center-symphony-konior-studio [access: 4.09.2019].
- *Gdansk Shakespearean Theatre/Renato Rizzi*, www.archdaily.com/595895/gdanskshakespearean-theatre-renato-rozzi [access: 24.09.2019].
- Franco J.T., *Video: Frei Otto's German Pavilion at Expo 67*, www.archdaily. com/607952/video-frei-otto-s-german-pavilion-at-expo-1967/ [access: 15.08.2015].
- Yunis Y., *Frei Otto and the Importance of Experimentation in Architecture*, www. archdaily.com/610531/frei-otto-and-the-importance-of-experimentation-in-architecture [access: 15.08.2015].
- *Lublin Science and Technology Park/Stelmach i Partnerzy Biuro Architektoniczne*, www.archdaily.com/614651/lublin-science-and-technology-park-stelmach-i-part nerzy-biuro-architektoniczne [access: 15.10.2019].
- Saieh N., *Multiplicity and Memory. Talking About Architecture with Peter Zumthor*, www.archdaily.com/85656/multiplicity-and-memory-talking-about-architecturewith-peter-zumthor [access: 18.02.2014].
- *Flyspot Warsaw/Biuro Projektow Lewicki Łatak*, www.archdaily.com/903172/ flyspot-warsaw-biuro-projektow-lewicki-latak [access: 3.10.2019].

Bibliography 189

- Mikulska K., *Sąd Rejonowy w Siedlcach*, www.architekturaibiznes.pl/architektura/prosze-wstac,1727.html [access: 19.09.2019].
- *Odkrywając fenomen La Tourette*, www.archsarp.pl/3387/odkrywajac-fenomen-latourette [access: 15.04.2020].
- *Gont i Beton*, www.bryla.pl/bryla/1,85298,6756638,Gont_i_Beton.html [access: 13.09.2019].
- D.L., *Zana House – milczący biurowiec*, www.bryla.pl/bryla/1,85301,7740864,Zana_House__milczacy_biurowiec.html [access: 23.09.2019].
- A.O., *Ascetyczne architektura z betonu I światła. Gmach Sądu w Siedlcach*, www.bryla.pl/bryla/56,85301,22968194,majestatyczny-sad-rejonowy-w-siedlcach.html [access: 19.09.2019].
- *Bałtyk w Poznaniu to najpiękniejszy budynek w Polsce*, www.bryla.pl/bryla/7,85301,21901211,baltyk-w-poznaniu-to-najpiekniejszy-budynek-w-polsce-oto.html [access: 18.09.2019].
- Leśnikowski W., *"Focusa" pokusa monumentalna*, www.budynekfocus.com/pl#www.budynekfocus.com/pl# [access: 23.09.2019].
- *O nas*, www.cricoteka.pl/pl/o-nas/ [access: 19.09.2019].
- *Nowa Żelazowa Wola. Piękna i nowoczesna!* 14.05.2010, www.domiporta.pl/poradnik/1,126867,7880998,Nowa_Zelazowa_Wola__Piekna_i_nowoczesna_.html [access: 27.12.2019].
- Bailey M., *The Bilbao Effect*, www.forbes.com/2002/02/20/0220conn.html [access: 5.04.2014].
- www.grupa5.com.pl/projekty/edukacja [access: 5.08.2019].
- *Manufaktura, Rewitalizacja*, www.manufaktura.com/site/479/powstanie-manufaktury/rewitalizacja [access: 9.12.2019].
- *The Krzysztof Penderecki European Centre for Music*, www.miesarch.com/work/606 [access: 6.12.2019].
- www.mocak.pl/nagrody-dla-obiektu [access: 20.09.2019].
- *Turystyka w Polsce. Systematycznie wzrasta liczba turystów w Toruniu*, www.money.pl/gospodarka/wiadomosci/artykul/turystyka;w;polsce;systematycznie;wzrasta;licz ba;turystow;w;toruniu,154,0,1523866.html [access: 14.09.2019].
- *Filharmonia Szczecińska. Ikona architektury i technika*, www.muratorplus.pl/inwestycje/inwestycje-publiczne/filharmonia-szczecinska-ikona-architektury-i-technika-aa-HH3i-QBw3-TDEW.html [access: 18.06.2020].
- www.muzeumlotnictwa.pl/gmach_muzeum/projekt.php [access: 3.12.2019].
- www.muzeumlotnictwa.pl/muzeum/pl/historia/ [access: 3.12.2019].
- www.mvrdv.nl/projects/51/baltyk?photo=5849 [access: 3.10.2019].
- Liczbarski M., *Budować z myślą o człowieku. An interview with Professor Marek Budzyński*, www.national-geographic.pl/ludzie/budowac-z-mysla-o-czlowieku-wywiad-z-prof-markiem-budzynskim [access: 6.11.2019].
- *Światowej sławy architekt odebrał nagrodę za warszawski projekt*, 26.06.2017, www.national-geographic.pl/ludzie/swiatowej-slawy-architekt-helmut-jahn-odebral-nagrode-za-warszawski-projekt-to-wyjatkowy-wklad-w-urbanistyczny-pejzaz-stolicy [access: 15.11.2019].
- *Trans World Airlines Flight Center (now TWA Terminal A) At New York International Airport*, Landmarks Preservation Commission, 19.07.1994, s. 7, www.neighborhoodpreservationcenter.org/db/bb_files/TWA023.pdf [access: 15.08.2015].

Bibliography

- Pogrebin R., *For First Time, Architect in China Wins Top Prize*, www.nytimes.com/2012/02/28/arts/design/pritzker-prize-awarded-to-wang-shu-chinese-architect.html [access: 12.11.2019].
- *The Pritzker Architecture Prize. Biography*, www.pritzkerprize.com/2015/biography [access: 15.08.2015].
- *The Pritzker Architecture Prize, Jury Citation Wang Shu*, www.pritzkerprize.com/jury-citation-wang-shu [access: 11.12.2019].
- *Aldo Rossi of Italy Elected 1990 Pritzker Architecture Prize Laureat*, www.pritzkerprize.com/laureates/1990# [access: 17.09.2019].
- *Konkurs Nagroda Roku SARP, edycja 2018*, www.sarp.org.pl/pokaz/konkurs_nagroda_roku_sarp-_edycja_2018,2569/ [access: 02.12.2019].
- *Nagroda Roku SARP wręczona!* www.sarp.org.pl/pokaz/nagroda_roku_sarp_wreczona!,1339/ [access: 02.12.2019].
- *Nagroda Roku – wyniki*, www.sarp.org.pl/pokaz/nagroda_roku-wyniki,2249/ [access: 14.09.2019].
- Bojańczyk A., *Siedziba Sądu Najwyższego*, www.sn.pl/osadzienajwyzszym/SitePages/Siedziba.aspx [access: 18.09.2019].
- *Centrum Spotkania Kultur. Historia*, www.spotkaniakultur.com/index.php/pl/o-csk [access: 18.11.2019].
- *Toruń na liście UNESCO*, www.torun.pl/pl/kultura/torun-na-liscie-unesco [access: 17.06.2019].
- *Toruń na liście UNESCO*, www.wizja.krakow.pl/pl/projects/41 [access: 19.09.2019].
- Bonowicz W., *Samolot, gołębica i Matka Boża*, www.wniebowstapienie.pl/parafia/historia/ [access: 28.10.2019].
- Ratajczak J., *Budowle nagrodzone w konkursie "Piękny Wrocław" – edycja XXIX*, www.wroclaw.pl/biznes/konkurs-piekny-wroclaw-edycja-xxix [access: 2.12.2019].
- *Frank Gehry A Sit-Down with the Artist of Architecture*, www.wsj.com/articles/SB10001424052748704474804576222872016570928 [access: 23.09.2016].
- Otto F., *The German Pavilon. Expo 1967*, www.youtube.com/watch?t=113&v=Z0mtFMoseUk [access: 15.08.2015].
- *Biblioteka Raczyńskich, Poznan. Strefa Przestrzeni*, www.youtube.com/watch?v=iNnDwEqu6o8 [access: 20.09.2019].
- *Hala Koszyki*, www.medusagroup.pl/projekty/handlowe/hala-koszyki-2/ [access: 20.09.2019].

Index

Note: Page numbers in *italics* indicate figures.

30 St Mary Axe 16
137kilo Architekci 128–129

acoustics: curvilinearity and 16, 41; form and 26; NOSPR building 35–36; Paris Philharmonic building 41; Rolex Learning Center 40; WOW effects and 35–36
Ad Artis Architects 120–121
Aedificium Anno Grand Prix 139
Age of Spectacle, The (Dyckhoff) 28
Agora Offices (Warsaw) *23*, 100, *100*, 101
AIA Gold Medal 30
Alberti, Leon Batista 19
Aldo Rossi Cemetery (Modena) 83
Alto, Alvaro 17
Andrä, Wolfhart 12
animation 13
APA Kuryłowicz & Associates 156, *156*, 157
Aplix (Le Cellier-sur-Loire) 16
Apple Store (New York) 59–60
appropriateness 58
Archiektura i wartość (*Architecture and Value*) (Basista) 52
Archigram group 13
Archistudio Studniarek + Pilinkiewicz 114, *114*, 115
Architect (Peltason and Ong-Yan) 177
architects: autonomy of thought 43, 177, 179; continuity of thought 42–43; creation of form 21–22, 26–27; creativity and 8–10, 19–21, 39–40, 54; design process 18–21, 36; economic and social conditions for 27; emotions and 36; inspiration and 24–25; knowing-in-action 21; rationalism and 36; reflection-in-action 21; search for originality 22–23; sensitivity to architecture 25–26; spirit of the age and 27; talent and 21; thought-sketches 20
Architectural Association (AA) 30
architectural space: combinational creativity and 39; creation of form and 26–27; defining 27–28; value and 52; value in 48, 52–54; *see also* space
architecture: art and 50–52, 175–177, 179; characteristics of 177; creative thought in 8–10; culture and 53; deconstructivism and 13; design tools and 10–11; economic dimension of 27, 53, 60; geometry and 8, 11–12, 14–15, 40; high-tech 13; historical elements of 83, 85, 177; interdisciplinarity and 12, 44n27; marketing and 16, 53, 60; matter in 6, 18; memory and 6; pattern in 14; place and time in 6–7, 58, 60; quality in 63; secessionist 73; sensitivity to 25–26; systematic planning in 10; technology and 9; thought in 6–7, 10; uniform language of forms in 11–12; use of computers in 10, 13; *see*

Index

also contemporary architecture; user-friendly architecture
Architecture Award (Chicago) 33
Architecture of the Year of the Silesian Voivodeship 137
Architektura i Biznes 88
Architektura-Murator 88, 101
Architizer A+ Award 131
Aristotle 177, 179
Arno, Anna 86n19
art: architecture and 50–52, 175–177, 179; beauty and 22–23; characteristics of 175–176; contemporary 50, 57; creativity and 38–39, 176; criticism and 176; direct pleasure and 175–176; emotions and 176, 179; expressive individuality in 176; historical elements of 177; idealism and 58; imagination and 177; intellectual challenge and 177; modernity in 2; novelty in 2; opera as 22–23; ready-made objects in 52; realistic 25; representation and 176; skill and virtuosity 176; style and 176; technical devices in 51–52; universal interpretation for 3
Art Instinct, The (Dutton) 3, 175
Art Nouveau 10
Association of Polish Architects 93
Atelier Loegler 152, *152*
ATI Design Group 130, *130*, 131
avant-garde architecture 13, 20

BAAS 62, 158, *158*, 159
Badowski, Zbigniew 70, 112, 138, 168, *168*, 169
Baltic (Poznan) 108, *108*, 109
Bank of Hong Kong 13
Bank of Shanghai (Hong Kong) 13
Barajas Airport (Madrid) 15–16
Barcelona Expo Pavilion 17
Barozzi, Fabrizio 54, *55*, 141
Barysz, Krzysztof 62, 136–137
Basista, Andrzej 52
Bauhaus building (Dessau) 27
Bauman, Zygmunt 86n19
beauty: appropriateness and 58; architectural 56–60; artificial 56–57; biological 56–57; classical art and 22–23; contemporary 58–60; culture and 56–58; curvilinearity and 36; importance of 56; as migrating category 57, 59; *parfois* 54; proportions and 58, 60; spirituality and 58–59; taking pleasure from 175–176; theory of 26; value and 52–53, 56–58
Behnisch, Günther 12
Berlin, Germany 14–15, 35
Bernini, Gian Lorenzo 16, 28
Best Building in Warsaw Award 101
Best Public Space of the Silesian Voivodeship 115
Beton 170
Białołeka Middle School and Cultural Center (Warsaw) 154, *154*, 155
Białystock: Czesław Niemen Amphitheatre 139; Podlaska Opera 138, *138*, 139
Bilbao Effect 14
BiM – Bulanda I Mucha Architekci 98–99
Biology and Nature 44n27
Biotowers 51
Biuro Projektów 76
Boden, Margaret 38–39
Body of the Year Award 107, 159
Bohlin Cywinski Jackson 59
Botta, Mario 15
BRE Bank (mBank) (Bydgoszcz) 60, 98, *98*, 99
BRT Architekten 17
Bruder Klaus Kapelle (Mechernich) 59
Bruegel the Elder 7
bubble houses 11, 43n16
Budzyński, Marek: on architectural beauty 26; Church of the Ascension of the Lord 168, *168*, 169; Podlaska Opera 138, *138*, 139; prizes and distinctions for 46n83; Supreme Court (Warsaw) 112–113; University of Warsaw Library 70–71
Bulanda, Andrzej 60, 99
Bydgoszcz: Brda waterfront in 99; BRE Bank (mBank) 60, 98, *98*, 99

Calatrava, Santiago 16
Campo Baeza, Alberto 15
Casa Olajossy ossia Villa (Fortezza) *22*
Casa Rotonda 15

Index 193

Castel del Monte of Lusatia 51–52
Center for the Meeting of Cultures
 (Lublin) 16, 65–66, *66*, 67, *67*
Center of Academic Information and the
 Academic Library (Katowice)
 162, *162*, 163
Centre National d'Art et de la Culture
 Georges Pompidou 13
ceramics 17, 45n57, 62, 73, 84, 159
Chieti 15
Chołdzyński, Andrzej M. 60, 96–97
Chopin, Fryderyk *24*, 127
Chopin Center (Warsaw) 126, *126*, 127,
 178
Chopin Museum (Żelazowa Wola) *24*,
 25, 74–75, *75*
Chopin Park (Żelazowa Wola) 74, *74*,
 75, *75*
churches: Church of the Ascension of
 the Lord 168–169; Church of
 the Holy Spirit 80–81; Higher
 Theological Seminary of the
 Resurrectionist Congregation
 22, 82–83; Votum Aleksa
 Chapel 170–171
Church of Santa Maria della Vittoria
 (Rome) 28
Church of the Ascension of the Lord
 (Warsaw) 168, *168*, 169
Church of the Holy Spirit (Tychy) 80,
 80, 81
CIAM 9
cities *see* urban space
Cities for People (Gehl) 63
civil engineering 2, 5n2, 11–12, 25, 107
combinational creativity 38
Commander's Cross of the Order of
 Polonia Restituta 46n83
commerce: Koszyki Hall 72, *72*, 73;
 Manufaktura Commerce Center
 76, *76*, 77, *77*
computers: architectural design and 10,
 13, 179; civil engineering and
 12; design process and 18–21;
 LED systems and 141; models
 and 19
concept 3, 41–42
conflict 42
contemporaneity: animation and 13;
 conflicts and 24; historical
 elements of 6, 78–79;
 innovativeness 48, 53, 60, 175;
 search for 14

contemporary architecture: creativity and
 38–39, 50; dematerialization of
 form and 28–29; emotions and
 179; historical elements of 6, 52;
 innovativeness in 6; materiality
 and 42; movement in 28; place
 in 3, 99; surprising 28–29, 31
contemporary art 50, 57–60
context 41–42, 64
Cooper Union (New York) 16, 29–31, 36
Copernicus Science Center (Warsaw)
 150, *150*, 151
courthouses: District Court (Katowice)
 114–115; Supreme Court
 (Warsaw) 112–113
Cracow: architectural meetings in
 27–28; Cricoteka Center 118,
 118, 119; Finance Faculty of the
 University of Economics 152,
 152, 153; Higher Theological
 Seminary of the Resurrectionist
 Congregation 22, 45n72, 82, *82*,
 83; Juliusz Słowacki Theatre 84;
 Małopolska Garden of Art 62,
 84, *84*, 85; Manggha Museum
 of Japanese Art and Technology
 54, *55*; Rocks Park 83;
 Voivodship Public Library 84
creativity: architect/designer 8–10,
 19–21, 39–40, 54; architectural
 form and 26–27; art and
 38–39, 176; combinational 38;
 contemporary architecture and
 8, 38–39; diversity and 38–43;
 emotions and 36; exploratory
 38; imagination and 38;
 rationalism and 36; relativity
 and 39; technology and 11;
 transformational 38–39
Creativity Code, The (Du Sautoy) 38
Cricoteka Center for the Documentation
 of the Art of Tadeusz Kantor
 (Cracow) 118, *118*, 119
Cricoteka Cricot 2 Theatre Center 119
cultural facilities: Center for the
 Meeting of Cultures 16, 65–67;
 Chopin Center 126–127;
 International Congress Center
 62, 78–79; Małopolska Garden
 of Art (Cracow) 62, 84–85;
 Shakespeare Theatre 130–131;
 Służewski House of Culture
 128–129

194 Index

culture: animation and 13; architecture and 6, 40, 53; beauty and 56–58; form and 42; innovativeness and 5n2; materials and 40, 42; philosophical 58; scientific 58; theological 58
curtain walls 16, 18, 42
curvilinear designs: acoustics and 16, 41; beauty and 36; Bilbao Effect and 14; emotions and 36; form and 15; innovation and 13; surprise and 36, 40; utilitarianism and 16; visibility and 16
Czesław Niemen Amphitheatre 139

Danielec, Tomasz 154
Davos Conference 5n2
DDJM Design Studio 134, *134*, 135
deconstructivism 13
Deleuze, Gilles 13
Deńko, Stanislaw 119
Derrida, Jacques 13
design process: architect/designer 18–21, 36; computerization and 18–21; continuity of thought in 42–43; designing solution 18; models and 19; research by design 19, 45n64; thought in 18–20; thought-sketches 20
Dessau Bauhaus building 27
Dissanayake, Ellen 176
District Court (Katowice) 114, *114*, 115
Doesburg, Theo van 9
Dolce Vita (1961) 10
Dominus Estate (California) 17
Domsta, Bazyli 122
Droszcz, Jacek 122
Duchamp, Marcel 176, 180n6
Duda, Andrzej 94, *94*, 95
Dunikowski, Marek 134
Dürer, Albrecht 56, 86n19
Du Sautoy, Marcus 38
Dutton, Denis 3, 14, 58, 62, 175–177
Dyckhoff, Tom 28–29, 53, 64
DZ Bank Building (Berlin) 14
Dzierżawski, Juliusz 73

ECHO (European Concert Hall Organization) 35
Ecstasy of Saint Theresa, The (Bernini) 28
ecstatic architecture 27–28

educational facilities: Białołeka Middle School and Cultural Center 154–155; Copernicus Science Center 150–151; Faculty of Neophilology and Applied Linguistics (University of Warsaw) 156–157; Finance Faculty of the University of Economics 152–153; Krzysztof Kieślowski Film School *61*, 62, 158–159
Eisenman, Peter 13
Ekielski, Władysław 153
Emerla, Arkadiusz 120
emotions 36, 176, 179
environment-friendly design 11
Estudio Barozzi Veiga 140, *140*, 141
European Association for Architectural Education (EAAE) 19, 45n64
European Rekula Project 50, 85n10
European Solidarity Center (Gdansk) 68, *68*, 69, *69*
European Union Prize for Contemporary Architecture 17
Expo Pavilion (Barcelona) 17
Eyck, Aldo van 9

F60 Project 51–52
Faculty of Neophilology and Applied Linguistics (University of Warsaw) 156, *156*, 157
Fallingwater (Pennsylvania) 7
Fellini, Federico 10
Ferdzynowie Design Studio 76
Finance Faculty of the University of Economics (Cracow) 152, *152*, 153
Fiszer, Stanisław 60, 96–97
Flyspot (Mory) 146, *146*, 147
Focus building (Warsaw) 92, *92*, 93
form: aerodynamics of 16; animation in 13; architect creation of 21–22, 26–27; concept and 41–42; conflict and 42; context and 41–42; creative imagination and 26; culture and 42; curvilinearity of 15–16; dematerialization of 28–29; formal laws and 27; function and 26, 41, 49, 60–61; geometrical haughtiness of 15–16; historical elements of 83; indifference and 41; innovativeness in 2, 6; models

Index 195

and 12; mutuality and 42; proportions and 58; quality of space and 63; relation with surroundings 60–61; simplicity of 33, 62; socioeconomic conditions and 27; softness in 40; spirit of the age and 27; technology in 2; uniform language of 11–12; use of computers in 13; utility and 28
Foster, Norman 13, 19, 28
Foster & Partners 16
F. Otto: The German Pavilion – Expo 1967 44n29
Friendly and Inclusive Space Award 137
Fryderyk Chopin National Institute 127
Fuller, Richard Buckminster 11
function: appropriateness and 58; architectural form and 26, 41, 49, 60–61, 83; beauty and 59–60; extended 53; public space and 64; value and 41, 52, 85

Gadamer, Hans-Georg 1, 26, 56, 58, 176
garden architecture 17
Gate No. 2 (Gdansk) 69
Gaudi, Antonio 36
Gdansk: European Solidarity Center 68, *68*, 69, *69*; Gate No. 2 69; Główne Miasto district 131; Monument of the Fallen Shipyard Workers 69; public space in 69; Shakespeare Theatre 130, *130*, 131; social rebellion in 69; Stare Przedmieście district 131; Wiadrownia district 123; World War II Museum 122–123
Gehl, Jan 63–64
Gehry, Frank 13–14, 16
Gelernter, Mark 26–27, 36
geo-domes 11
geometry: architectural 2, 8, 11, 14–15, 40; haughtiness and 15–16; materiality and 40–41; models and 12; rationalism and 36; right-angle 1, 35–36; surprising 28–29
German architecture 12
German pavilion (World Expo:1967) 12, 44n29
Gesamtkuntswerk 54

Ghetto Heroes Monument 32
Gloria Artis Silver Medal for Merit to Culture 46n79, 46n81
Graaf, Reiner de 38
Grassi, Giorgio 15
Grimshaw, Nicholas 13
Gropius, Walter 9, 27
Grupa 5 Architekci 62, 158, *158*, 159
Guggenheim Museum (New York) 7–8, 43n5

Hadid, Zaha 13, 20, 38
Hearst headquarters (New York) 16, 28
Helmcke, Johann-Gerhard 44n27
Herman, Dariusz 162
Herzog, Jacques 16–17
Higher Theological Seminary of the Resurrectionist Congregation (Cracow) 22, 45n72, 82, *82*, 83
Hollein, Hans 21
Hong Kong 13
Hotel Andels (Łódź) 76–77
HS99 162–163
Hundertwasser (Vienna) 10

IBA Program (Internationale Bauastellung Fuerst Pueckerland) 50–52, 85n10
iconicity 8, 12, 14, 99
Icon of Architecture 155
idealism 9
Ilmurzyńska, Krystyna 70, 138
imagination 16, 19, 26–27, 38, 177
Inarko 94, *94*
indifference 41
industrial buildings: architecture of 53; innovativeness in 16–17; marketing and 16, 53; pragmatic spatial solutions in 16; transformation of 34, 69, 77–79; value and 52–53; as works of art 51–52; *see also* post-industrial transformation
Ingarden, Krzysztof 84
Ingarden, Roman 58, 60
Ingarden & Ewý Architects 62, 84, *84*
innovativeness: confirmation of 3; criteria for 3; curtain wall materiality and 16, 42; defining 2; ecstatic forms and 28–29; expressionist tendencies 2; forms of 1–2; historical buildings and 6; intellectual

stage 2; mesh lathing and 50;
post-war German architecture
and 12; social stage 3; technical
stage 2
In Search of Beauty 56, 86n19
International, The (2009) 43n5
International Biennale of Young
Architects in Minsk 155
International Congress Center
(Katowice) 62, 78–79, *79*
Isozaki, Arata 54, *55*
Ito, Toyo 42

Jagiełło, Olgierd 72, 100
Jagiełłowicz, Piotr 120
Jahn, Helmut 22, 53, 179
Jałowiecki, Bohdan 63
Jan Baptysta Quadro Award 109, 121
Japanese architecture 10
JEMS architects: Agora Offices *23*,
100–101; credo of 24–25;
International Congress Center
62, 78, *79*; Koszyki Hall 72, *72*,
73; Raczyński Library 164–165
Jencks, Charles 8–10, 28
Jordanki Cultural and Congress Center
(Toruń) 142, *142*, 143, 174n49
Juliusz Słowacki Theatre (Cracow) 84
Juzwa, Nina 85n10

Kahn, Louis 9
Kandinsky, Wassily 8
Kant, Immanuel 58, 177
Kantor, Tadeusz 119
Kaponiera Roundabout 109
Karol Szymanowski Academy of
Music 137
Kasinowicz, Wojtek 120
Katowice: Academy of Music in
137; Center of Academic
Information and the Academic
Library 162, *162*, 163;
Culture Zone 34, 78–79, *79*,
163; District Court 114, *114*,
115; Hornbeam Labyrinth
78; International Congress
Center 62, 78–79, *79*; Karol
Szymanowski Academy
of Music 137; Krzysztof
Kieślowski Film School 158,
158, 159; Małeccy Design
Studio 62; mining industry
in 34–35, 78; NOSPR

building 29, 34, *34*, 35, *35*,
36, *37*, 46n81, 78, *79*; Plan
of Great 78; post-industrial
transformation in 34, *51*, 52;
public space in 78–79; Silesian
Acropolis 35; Silesian Museum
51, 52, 78, *79*; Silesian Spodek
35, 62, 78; Symfonia Center of
Musical Science and Education
34, 62, 136–137; University of
Economics 163; University of
Silesia 78, 159, 163
Katowice Central Park 78
Katowice Mine 78
knowing-in-action 21
Konior, Tomasz: Białołęka Middle
School and Cultural Center
154–155; on complexity in
architecture 179; Katowice
Culture Zone 78, *79*; NOSPR
building 34–35, *37*; prizes
and distinctions for 46n81; on
sensitivity in architecture 25;
State Music School No. 1 *25*;
Symfonia Center of Musical
Science and Education 62,
136–137
Konior Studio 34, *37*, 62, 78, *79*,
136, 154
Koszyki Hall (Warsaw) 72, *72*, 73
Kowalewski, Zbigniew 122–123
Kozłowski, Dariusz: on architect ideas
20; on architectural studies 23;
Casa Olajossy ossia Villa *22*;
Higher Theological Seminary
22, 45n72, 82, *82*, 83; on opera
22–23; on search for originality
14, 22–23
Kozłowski, Tomasz *22*
Krzysztof Kieślowski Film School
(Katowice) *61*, 62, 158,
158, 159
Krzysztof Penderecki European Center
for Music (Lusławice) 134,
134, 135
Kubec, Jan 150, *150*, 151
Kuhn, Rolf 85n10
Kuma, Kengo 17, 25
Kuryłowicz, Stefan 93
Kuryłowicz & Associates 92, *92*,
106–107
Kutniowski, Jarosław 134
Kutz, K. 47n101

Kwadrat Design Studio 122–123
Kwieciński, Andrzej 122
Laboratorium Architektury RAr2 150
La Cité de la Musique (Paris) 41
Lahdelma, Ilmari 32
Laskowski, Wojciech 93
Łatak, Kazimierz 146–147
La Tourette Priory 7, 40
Lausanne, France 39–40
Leach, Neil 28
Le Cellier-sur-Loire, France 16
Le Corbusier: La Tourette Priory 7; modernist architecture and 7, 9, 15, 52; *The Modulor* 7; Notre Dame du Haut pilgrim chapel 7
Leonardo Award 155
Leonhardt, Fritz 12
Leśniewski, Stanisław 71
Levinson, Jerrold 177
Lewicki, Piotr 146–147
Leykam, Marek 109
Libeskind, Daniel 13
libraries: Center of Academic Information and the Academic Library 162–163; Raczyński Library 164–165; University of Warsaw Library 70–71; Voivodship Public Library 84
Lieben-Seutter, Christoph 47n102
Life Between Buildings (Gehl) 63
Life in Architecture award 103, 131, 151
Lloyd's building (London) 13
Łódź: Hotel Andels 76–77; Manufaktura Commerce Center 76, *76*, 77, *77*; MS² Museum of Art 76–77; public space in 77
Loegler, Romuald 153
logic 10
London: 30 St Mary Axe 16; Architectural Association (AA) 30; Lloyd's building 13; Royal Academy of Arts 28
London City Hall 16
Louis Vuitton headquarters (Osaka) 17
Lower Lusatia: Castel del Monte of Lusatia 51–52; F60 Project 51–52; mining industry in 3, 5n10, 50; post-industrial transformation in 3, 50–51
Lublin: Center for the Meeting of Cultures 16, 65–66, *66*, 67, *67*; public space in 66–67;

Science and Technology Park 104, *104*, 105; Theatre Under Construction 66; Zana House 102, *102*, 103
Luft, Andrzej 169
Łukasiewicz, Jan 71
Lusławice, Krzysztof Penderecki European Center for Music 134–135
Lutomski, Jerzy 76
Lutyens, E. 27
Lynn, Greg 13

Madrid Barajas Airport 15–16
Magma Art and Congress 174n49
Mahlamäki, Rainer 32
Mahlamäki and Lahdelma Architects 32–33
Main Prize of the European Commercial Prosperity Awards 46n81
Majkusiak, Paweł 72
Małeccy Design Studio 62, 158, *158*, 159
Malewicz, Kazimierz 38
Małopolska Garden of Art (Cracow) 62, 84, *84*, 85
Malraux, André 20
Manggha Museum of Japanese Art and Technology (Cracow) 54, *55*
manifests 10
Manufaktura Commerce Center (Łódź) 76, *76*, 77, *77*
marketing 16, 53, 60
Masłowski, Tomasz 137
Massif Centrale, France 7
materiality: complicated geometry and 40–41; concept and 42; contemporary 60; curtain walls and 16, 42; curvilinearity and 16; elevations and 17–18, 42; glass in 67; industrial structures 16–17; lightness and 17–18; multi-layered curtain walls 16, 18; new materiality and 15–17; Paris Philharmonic building 40–41; technological solutions and 16–17, 58, 60; transparency and 16–18; urban landscape and 28
materials: ceramics and 17, 45n57, 73, 84, 159; cladding and 31, 41; culture and 40, 42; curvilinear designs 16; mesh lathing 50; new materiality

198 Index

and 15–17; poured-in-place concrete 83; stone and 17–18, 40, 45n57; symbolism of 50; technologically advanced 16–17; traditional 17
matter 6, 18
Mayne, Thom 30
mBank *see* BRE Bank (mBank)
Medal of the Centenary of the Regaining of Polish Independence 46n81
Medusa Group 72, *72*, 73
memory 6, 54, 57, 62
Men in Black (1997) 43n5
Menis, Fernando 142, *142*, 143
Mercury Hotel (Warsaw) 107
Metropolitan Museum of Art (New York) 8
Meuron, Pierre de 16–17
Michelangelo Buonarroti 26, 56, 177
Miecznikowski, Wojciech 134
Mieczysław Karłowicz Philharmonic (Szczecin) 54, 140, *140*, 141
Mies van der Rohe, Ludwig 9, 17, 59
Mies van der Rohe Award: BRE Bank building 99; Chopin Center 127; Copernicus Science Center 151; District Court 115; European Union Prize for Contemporary Architecture 17; Krzysztof Kieślowski Film School 159; Krzysztof Penderecki European Center for Music 135; Mieczysław Karłowicz Philharmonic 54, *55*, 141; Shakespeare Theatre 131; Symfonia Center of Musical Science and Education 137; Votum Aleksa Chapel 171; Warsaw Stock Exchange 97; World War II Museum 123; Żelazowa Wola restoration 75
Miłobędzki, Maciej 72, 100
Minister of Internal Affairs and Administration 95
Misiągiewicz, Maria 22, 45n72, 82, *82*, 83
Möbius House 13
models 12, 19
modernism: architecture and 14; in art 2; concept and 41; creativity and 8; cult of the machine and 9; idealism and 9; Le Corbusier and 7, 9, 15, 52; mass production and 17;

submissiveness to the past in 9–10; Wright and 7–8
Modern Movements in Architecture (Jencks) 9–10
Modulor, The (Le Corbusier) 7
Mondrian, Piet 8
Monument of the Fallen Shipyard Workers 69
Morphosis Architects 30
Mory: Flyspot 146–147; Lewicki Łatak Design Studio 146, *146*
Mostafa, Marcin 128
MS^2 Museum of Art (Łodź) 76–77
Mucha, Włodzimierz 60, 99
Mulhouse-Brunstatt, France 16
Munich Olympic Stadium 12
Museum of Imagination 20
museums: Chopin Museum 25, 74–75; Chopin Park 74–75; Cricoteka Center for the Documentation of the Art of Tadeusz Kantor 119; European Solidarity Center 68–69; POLIN Museum of the History of Polish Jews 16, 29, 32–33, 36; Porta Posnania (ICHOT) 120–121; Silesian Museum 52, 78, *79*; World War II Museum 122–123
music: architecture and 25, 49, 179; exploratory creativity and 38; NOSPR building 34–35, 47n102; Oslo Opera House 48–49; romantic trend in 39; Scharoun Philharmonic 35; Symfonia Concert Hall 34
music centers: Jordanki Cultural and Congress Center 142–143; Krzysztof Penderecki European Center for Music 134–135; Mieczysław Karłowicz Philharmonic 54, 140–141; NOSPR building 34–35, 78; Podlaska Opera 138–139; Symfonia Center of Musical Science and Education (Katowice) 34, 62, 136–137
mutuality 42
MVRDV 108–109
Myjak, Adam 71

National Symphonic Orchestra of the Polish Radio (NOSPR) *see* NOSPR building
Nawara, Piotr 118–119

Neff, Edwin Wallace 11
new materiality 15–16
New Museum of Contemporary Art (New York) 3, 48–50, 62
New York: Apple Store 59–60; Cooper Union 16, 29–31, 36; Guggenheim Museum 7–8, 43n5; Hearst headquarters 16, 28; Metropolitan Museum of Art 8; New Museum of Contemporary Art 3, 48–50, 62; New York by Gehry 16; TWA Flight Center 11–12; WTC Transportation Hub 16
New York by Gehry 16
NIAiU team 4
Niemczyk, Stanisław 35, 81
Ningbo History Museum 18
NO – Natkaniec, Olechnicki Architekci 108–109
NOSPR building (Katowice): acoustics in 35; Culture Zone and 34, 78, *79*; European classical music community and 47n102; exterior *35*; floor plan *34*; grand concert hall *37*; prizes and distinctions for 35, 46n81; public space and 78; right-angle geometry and 35; transformation of industrial site for 34–35; Wow effect and 29, 36
Notre Dame du Haut pilgrim chapel 7
Nouvel, Jean 40–41
novelty 2
Nowosielski, Jerzy 81
Nsmoonstudio 118

office buildings: Agora Offices (Warsaw) *23*, 100–101; Baltic (Poznan) 108–109; BRE Bank (mBank) 60, 98–99; Focus building (Warsaw) 92–93; Q22 (Warsaw) 106–107; Science and Technology Park (Lublin) 104–105; Social Insurance Building (Zabrze) 94–95; Warsaw Stock Exchange 60, 96–97; Zana House (Lublin) 102–103
Officer's Cross of the Order of Polonia Restituta 46n79
Okrąglak (Poznan) 109
Olympic Stadium (Munich) 12
OMA design studio 50

Ong-Yan, Grace 177
On the Art of Building in Ten Books (Alberti) 19
OP Architekten 76
Oslo, Finland 48–49
Oslo Opera House 3, 48–49
Ostrogski Castle 127
Otto, Frei 12, 44n27

parametric architecture 12
Parc de la Villette 40–41
Paris, France: La Cité de la Musique 41; Le Centre Pompidou 13; Parc de la Villette 40–41; Paris beltway 41; Philharmonic building 39–41; Sainte Chappelle 59
Paris Philharmonic building 39–41
Pascal, Yannick 76
Paszkowska, Natalia 128
Paszkowski, Zbigniew 53
patterns 14, 21
Peak Hong-Kong club 20
Pearl in the Crown (1971) 47n101
Peltason, Ruth 177
Penderecki, Krzysztof 135
People's Bazaar (Warsaw) 73
Perrault, Dominique 16
Perret, August 9
Piano, Renzo 13
Piątek, Grzegorz 71
Pietà (Michelangelo) 56
Pivot, Jean-Marc 76
place: architectural value and 54; in architecture 6–7; beauty and 54, 56; culture of time and 58, 60; form and 61; history and 54, 62; space and 62–63; urban space and 64, 67; user-friendly architecture and 48–52; values of 63
Plan of Great Katowice 78
Plato 179
Podlaska Opera (Białystock) 138, *138*, 139
POLIN Museum of the History of Polish Jews (Warsaw) 16, 29, 32, *32*, 33, *33*, 36
Polish architecture: churches 90, 168–171; commerce 72–73, 76–77, 90; courthouses 89, 112–115; cultural facilities 16, 62, 65–67, 78–79, 84–85, 89, 126–131; educational facilities 89, 150–159; houses of music

89, 134–143; libraries 70–71, 90, 162–165; museums 89, 118–123; office buildings 88, 92–109; postmodernism and 83; Pritzker Prize and 54; public utility buildings 4, 14, 71, 88; reinterpretation of heritage in 64; sports facilities 89, 146–147
Polish Cement in Architecture 93, 113, 115, 121, 155
Polish National Radio Symphony Orchestra 34–35, *37*, 47n102; *see also* NOSPR building
Polish Underground State 113
Polityka 119, 129
Popławski, Wojciech 76
Porębska, Ewa P. 64
Porta Posnania (ICHOT) (Poznan) 120, *120*, 121
Posnanski, Israel 77
post-industrial transformation: in Katowice 34, *51*, 52; Lauchhammer coking plant 51; in Lower Lusatia 3, 50–52; NOSPR building and 34; user-friendly architecture in 48, 50–52
postmodernism 40, 83
Poznan: Baltic 108, *108*, 109; International Fairgrounds 109; Kaponiera Roundabout 109; *Okrąglak* 109; Porta Posnania (Ichot) 120–121; Raczyński Library 164, *164*, 165
PPW Fort Architektura 68, *69*
Prescott, John 29
Pritzker Prize: Aldo Rossi (1990) 15; Arata Isozaki (2019) 54, *55*; architect autonomy of thought and 43, 177; architectural distinction and 54; Peter Zumthor (2009) 59; public awareness of architecture through 21; SANNA architects (2010) 50; Thom Mayne (2005) 30; Wang Shu (2012) 18
Prize of the Minister of Infrastructure 101, 113
Prize of the Minister of Investment and Economic Development 107
Prize of the Minister of National Heritage 46n81
proportions 58, 60

Proust, Marcel 59
public space: accessible 49–50; architectural beauty and 60; Center for the Meeting of Cultures 67; functions of 64; monumental architecture in 49, 67, 69; place and 49–50, 67; transformation of 66–67, 69, 71, 73–75, 77–79; *see also* urban space
public utility buildings: architecture of 4, 46n83; financing of 88; formal solutions for 71; materials and 45n57; patterns in 14; Polish architecture and 4, 14, 71, 88; user-friendly 71

Q22 (Warsaw) 106, *106*, 107
quality 63

Raczynski, Edward 165
Raczyński Library (Poznan) 164, *164*, 165
Rashtrapati Bhavan (Viceroy's House) (New Delhi) 27
rationalism 36
realistic art 25
reflection-in-action 21
relations 13
research by design 19, 45n64
Ricola Europe candy factory (Mulhouse-Brunstatt) 16
Riegler Riewe Architekten *51*, 78, *79*
Rizzi, Renato 130, *130*, 131
Rocks Park (Cracow) 83
Rogers, Everett M. 2
Rogers, Richard 13, 15
Rolex Learning Center (Lausanne) 39–40
Ronchamp, France 7
Rossi, Aldo 14–15
Rottenberg, Anda 57–58, 86n19
Rowińska, Marta 170–171
Rowiński, Lech 170–171
Royal Academy of Arts (London) 28

Saarinen, Eero 11–12
Sadowski, Marcin 72, 100
Sainte Chappelle (Paris) 59
Saint-Marie-de-la-Tourette Priory Eveux-Sur-Abresle *see* La Tourette Priory
SANAA Design Studios 40, 48–49

Index 201

San Cataldo Cemetery (Moderna) 15
San Fermin Public School 15
Sant Elia, Antonio 20
SARP Awards 93, 95, 99, 119, 135, 137, 143, 159
SARP Design of the Year Award 33
SARP Honorary Award 22, 45n72, 46n79, 46n83, 99, 127, 153
Scharoun Philharmonic (Berlin) 35
Scheler, Max 58
Science and Technology Park (Lublin) 104, *104*, 105
Scott Brown, Denise 49
Sendai Mediatheque (Japan) 21
Shakespeare Theatre (Gdansk) 130–131
Siegel, Curt 11
Silesia: architecture in 25, 62, 79, 86n37, 95; mining industry in 62, 78; *see also* Katowice
Silesian Acropolis (Katowice) 35
Silesian Museum (Katowice) *51*, 52, 78, *79*
Silesian Quality Award 46n81
Silesian School Architects 25
Spodek (Katowice) 35, 62, 78
Silesian Voivode 95
Służewski House of Culture (Warsaw) 128, *128*, 129
Słyk, Jan 19
Śmierzewski, Piotr 162
Snøhetta 48–49
Social Insurance Building (Zabrze) 94, *94*, 95
space: accessible 49; architectural form and 26–27; between buildings 63; cities and 62–63; contemporary architecture and 27; defining 63, 86n40; geometry and 39; place and 62–65, 67; value and 52–54; *see also* public space; urban space
Special Award of the President of Gdansk 123
spirituality 58–59
sports facilities: Flyspot 146–147; Olympic Stadium (Munich) 12; Silesian Spodek 62
State Music School No. 1 (Warsaw) 25
Stefański, Wacław 22, 45n72, 82, *82*, 83
Stelmach, Bolesław: Center for the Meeting of Cultures 66–67, *67*;
Chopin Center 126–127, *178*; Chopin Museum *24*, 25; Chopin Park 74, *74–75*; prizes and distinctions for 46n79; Science and Technology Park 104, *104*, 105; Zana House 102–103
Stelmach & Partners Architectural Office 66, *67*, 74, 102, 104, *104*, 126
Stirling, James 9
stone 17–18, 40, 45n57
Stryjeński, Tadeusz 153
Subalski, Wojciech 162
SUD Architectes 76, *77*
Sukiennik, Jan 128
Supreme Court (Warsaw) 112, *112*, 113
surprise: in architecture 24; contemporary architecture and 39; curvilinearity and 36, 40; diversity and 38–40; ecstatic forms and 28; innovativeness and 2; Wowhaus and 29–30
Swiss Federal Institute of Technology 40
Symfonia Center of Musical Science and Education (Katowice) 34, 62, 136, *136*, 137
Szczecin, Mieczysław Karłowicz Philharmonic 54, *55*, 140, *140*, 141
Szczepanik-Dzikowski, Jerzy 72–73, 100
Szultk, Agnieszka 118–119
Świętorzecki, Mateusz 72

Tange, Kenzo 10
Targowski, Wojciech 68, *69*
Tarkovsky, Andrei 25
Tarnów upon the Vistula, Votum Aleksa Chapel 170, *170*, 171
Tarski, Alfred 71
Tatarkiewicz, Władysław 57–58
team design 10
technology: construction and 9; creativity and 11; environment-friendly 11; innovativeness and 2; new materiality and 16–17, 58, 60
theater of the imagination 177
Theatre Under Construction 66
Thermal Baths (Vals) 39–40
Thorsen, Kjetil T. 49
thought: architectural 6–7, 10, 18; continuity of 42–43; design

process and 18–19; modern architecture and 9 thought-sketches 20
Three Days of the Condor (1975) 43n5
Tobias Grau 17
Toruń: Jordanki Cultural and Congress Center 142–143; Old Town 143
Toyo Ito & Associates 21
transformational creativity 38–39
Tschumi, Bernard 41, 53, 61–62
Tuan, Yi Fu 63
Tulkowska-Słyk, Karolina 2
TWA Flight Center (New York) 11–12, 15
Twardowski, Kazimierz 71, 83
Tychy, Church of the Holy Spirit 80, *80*, 81

UIA Medal 75
umbrellas 12
UNESCO World Heritage list 7, 143
University of Silesia *61*, 78, 159, 163
University of Warsaw Library 70, *70*, 71
UN Studio 13
urban density 20
urban space: building form and 60–61; decreasing car traffic in 63; development of 63; elevation of value and 62; freedom and 62; functions of 64; monumental architecture in 49, 67, 69; place in 64, 67; Polish economy and 60; public utility buildings 71; taming of 3; value of 62–65; vitality and 64
user-friendly architecture: New Museum of Contemporary Art 49–50; Oslo Opera House 48–49; place and 48–52; post-industrial transformation and 48, 50–52; utility and 53–54; value and 52–54, 64
utility 52–54, 58, 60

Vacheron Constantin factory 53
Vals Thermal Baths 39–40
value: architectural space and 48, 52–54; beauty and 52–53, 56–58; cultural and artistic 52–53; duration of 53–54; *Gesamtkuntswerk* 54; hierarchy of 58; industrial buildings and 52–53; urban space and 62–65; user-friendly architecture and 52–54, 64; utility and 52–54
Veiga, Alberto 54, *55*, 141
Viceroy's House (Rashtrapati Bhavan) (New Delhi) 27
Voivodship Public Library (Cracow) 84
Votum Aleksa Chapel (Tarnów) 170, *170*, 171

Wang Shu 18
Warsaw: Agora Offices *23*, 100, *100*, 101; Białołeka Middle School and Cultural Center 154–155, *155*; Chopin Center 126–127, *178*; Church of the Ascension of the Lord 168, *168*, 169; Copernicus Science Center 150–151; Faculty of Neophilology and Applied Linguistics (University of Warsaw) 156, *156*, 157; Focus building 92, *92*, 93; Ghetto Heroes Monument 32; Koszuki Hall 72, *72*, 73; Mercury Hotel 107; Ostrogski Castle 127; POLIN Museum of the History of Polish Jews 16, 29, 32, *32*, 33, *33*, 36; public space in 71, 73; Q22 106, *106*, 107; Służewski House of Culture 128–129; State Music School No. 1 *25*; Supreme Court 112, *112*, 113; University of Warsaw Library 70, *70*, 71; Warsaw Stock Exchange 60, 96, *96*, 97
Warsaw-Friendly Building award 157
Warsaw Stock Exchange 60, 96, *96*, 97
Warsaw Uprising monument 113
Wdowski, Dominik 139
Wizja Stanisław Deńko Design Studio 118
Wojda, Maciej 120
World Museum of Imagination 62
World War II Museum (Gdansk) 122, *122*, 123
WOW effects 29, 33, 35–36
Wowhaus: Cooper Union 29–31, 36; innovativeness and 29, 36; NOSPR building 29, 34–36; POLIN Museum 29, 32–33, *33*, 36
Wright, Frank Lloyd 7–8

WTC Transportation Hub (New York) 16
WWAA 128–129

Xenakis, Iannis 7

Zabrze: Social Insurance Building 94,
  94, 95; ZUS Building 95
Zana House (Lublin) 102, *102*, 103

Zeki, Semir 56, 86n19
Żelazowa Wola: Chopin Museum *24*, 25,
  74–75, *75*; Chopin Park 74, *74*,
  75, *75*; public space in 74–75
Znak 86n19
Zubel, Henryk 94, *94*, 95
Zumthor, Peter 39–40, 42, 59, 63
ZUS Building 95

Taylor & Francis eBooks

www.taylorfrancis.com

A single destination for eBooks from Taylor & Francis with increased functionality and an improved user experience to meet the needs of our customers.

90,000+ eBooks of award-winning academic content in Humanities, Social Science, Science, Technology, Engineering, and Medical written by a global network of editors and authors.

TAYLOR & FRANCIS EBOOKS OFFERS:

- A streamlined experience for our library customers
- A single point of discovery for all of our eBook content
- Improved search and discovery of content at both book and chapter level

REQUEST A FREE TRIAL
support@taylorfrancis.com